GIOVANNI PISANO · SCULPTOR

FRONTISPIECE: Miriam or Mary, Sister of Moses (Detail)
From the Siena Cathedral façade:
See note on page 216

MICHAEL AYRTON

GIOVANNI PISANO

SCULPTOR

Introduction by HENRY MOORE

Photographs specially taken by Ilario Bessi
in collaboration with Henry Moore

With 370 black and white plates and a color frontispiece

WEYBRIGHT AND TALLEY
NEW YORK

To the memory of Hans Gronau
who with Dr Hanna Kiel
first showed me the sculpture of the Pisani
in 1947

Published in the United States by Weybright and Talley, Inc.
3 East 54th Street, New York, New York 10022.

Library of Congress Catalog Card Number: 75-87066

Printed in West Germany

Contents

Introduction by Henry Moore

THE FIRST TIME I saw the sculptures of Giovanni Pisano was in 1925 when I visited Pisa on a travelling scholarship from the Royal College of Art. I must only have been able to admire, or try to admire, the sculptures on the façade and those on the top of the Baptistry, with struggle and effort, for when I could only see them at such a distance above me it was impossible to feel the true three-dimensional, face-to-face relationship which I need from sculpture. I wanted to see them as Giovanni made them, because a sculptor cannot work with a long arm and a long chisel from the ground and carve something up in the air; he must carve it in his studio as a man-to-man relationship. It was only after the war, when the big figures from the niches were taken down and put inside the Baptistry, that I saw them near-to, and then I was at once struck by the tremendous dramatic force of what I would call the hallmark of Giovanni's sculptural quality, style, or personality. It was also after the war that I saw properly the smaller life-size figures which, for their preservation, have been removed from the architecture and put into the Pisa Museum. Then I saw in so many of them the thrusting-forward neck, the neck that goes forward at an angle of forty-five degrees or even more (but with the head itself left upright). It has been said that he carved them like that to avoid a squat, foreshortened appearance when the figure was to be seen high up in perspective, but you get the same urgent, thrusting attitude in some of his figures which are meant to be seen at eye-level, such as the Caritas on the Pisa Cathedral pulpit. This thrust, I think, was something Giovanni felt about the urgency of human communication. He simply felt that the figure needed this tremendously potent gesture forward to 'give the message'. These sculptures are absolute presences and they made a lasting, most powerful impression on me.

Not only the figures in the Pisa Museum but, later, the Siena Cathedral façade sculptures proved to me that Giovanni Pisano was a great sculptor in every sense, particularly in the sense of understanding and using three-dimensional forms to affect people, to portray human feelings and character, to express great truths.

The surprising thing was to find how Giovanni had freed himself from his father Nicola. I had been taught and, later, when I was teaching, I repeated that the father of the Renaissance was Nicola Pisano and that Giovanni, his son, was his follower. Nicola, I presume, took his start from Roman sarcophagus reliefs which freed him from the Byzantine stiffness and gave him a naturalistic, more realistic, point of view about sculpture than his predecessors. But Giovanni went further; what he did was really to articulate the individual parts of the human body. I think it was Giovanni Pisano's excitement over articulating the human body in sculpture, *in a way that we know from our own physical experience that it can't articulate*, that made his sculpture new and great; we know that the head is a separate movable unit, the neck is another unit, the shoulders are another, the pelvis is another, the legs can bend at the knees and then bend at the feet. There are about sixteen individual units in the human figure: head, neck, thorax, pelvis, thighs, lower legs, feet, arms and hands all of which can bend at angles to each other. Having these units, you can place them at different angles in space. Take Giovanni's so-called 'dancing figure': look at that forward-thrusting neck, that vertical head; the body sways so that the hips are pushed forward and the legs are held back. I don't think it was meant to be a figure that was actually dancing; I think he was giving energy to the figure by articulating it from inside. His father's sculptures, wonderful as they are, are often very static and rigid. They do not have what I was searching for when I was a young sculptor, the using of real three-dimensional forms poised in space. Nicola Pisano did not use the human body as he used facial expression, and you have to use the body as you use the face if you want really to convey the fullest human meaning. This is something which Michelangelo did later on. He used the body to express his deep philosophical understanding of human nature, human tragedy and everything else. In this Giovanni had been the innovator.

But if I compare Michelangelo's David with Giovanni Pisano's figure of David from the Siena façade, I find that although the David of Michelangelo is an unbelievable, superhuman achievement for a young man of twenty-five, it is very different as an expression of a philosophical outlook on life; it is a marvellously realistic understanding of a young man's body, a body exuding tremendous physical assurance... The David of Giovanni Pisano has behind it an intensity of human understanding, of deep personality; it's like comparing Benedick and Hamlet. The Giovanni Pisano has all the implications of the contradictions, troubles and worries inside its head that Hamlet had, whereas the Michelangelo has no real troubles in its head at all, no unconquerable problems.

I have said that by making the pieces of the human body seem movable and articulated with one another, you give sculpture intensity, but by this I do not mean the portraying of actual physical

Fig. w, pl. 105

Fig. u

Fig. y

Fig. s, pl. 136

Fig. a

movement such as walking, running etc. For Giovanni gets drama into his figures when they stand still, as Masaccio did later. In Masaccio's *The Tribute Money* you feel, when Peter hands over the money, that there is a kind of electric charge in the air and this is created not by strong physical action but by a dramatic tension, something that both Masaccio and Giovanni could give in their work. The late Michelangelo has the same thing. In the *Rondanini Pietà* you get an absolute volte-face from his early David, through an almost expressionist antirealistic use of anatomy. It's a change from the Renaissance back to the Gothic. It's as if Michelangelo had come through at the end of his life to something nearer to Giovanni's attitude. It's the huge difference between using anatomy for its own sake and using a knowledge of the human figure to express one's philosophy, one's interpretation of life generally – and this is what surprises me: that Giovanni had done this so early. This is why I think he should be more widely recognized now as the great artist that he is. When you look at Giovanni's relief carvings, it is natural to relate them to Giotto's frescoes. So many people think that Giotto was the forerunner of the Renaissance, that he changed Italian art by using the human figure in a plastic way to express human emotions, but Giovanni was doing this earlier; for instance those triangular eyes with which Giotto expressed terrific grief can be found in Giovanni's *Massacre of the Innocents* on the Pistoia pulpit. But all this does not impress me as much as the single figures I first mentioned. For me, it is possible to separate his narrative, his story-telling gift, from his gift for form, which is why to me the single figures are the most exciting.

I want to say something about stone and marble carving as a technical thing. For instance, if you carve a piece of marble freshly quarried, it is much softer than it will be a year or two later. When it is new, it is called 'green' (like a green tree with the sap in it), and a stone used quickly out of a quarry is twice as easy to cut and to carve as stone which has been quarried a few years. I think that having his quarry near Pisa would mean that the marble would be used very soon after being quarried. Then, again, I think Giovanni had better-tempered tools than his predecessors. This would have given him more speed and freedom than his father. He would not have taken half as long to block out a big mass, and then to articulate it into his smaller masses. This could be one of the explanations for his freedom in the use of stone compared to other sculptors before him. Of course there's a difference in the hardness of various stones, but even this relates to its time of quarrying. This applies even to very hard stones like granite. The granite in Cornwall is worked into kerb-stones and cobble-stones immediately it is quarried, and while it is 'green'. Giovanni's marble from San Giuliano wasn't all that hard, which is why his exterior sculptures are so weathered. I don't think we lose anything essential by that weathering. I even think the weathering reveals the big, simple design of his forms more clearly. It probably reduces what we see to what it had been a stage before it was finished, simplifying it back again without the detail.

Nicola Pisano used the drill as part of his studio technique because with the drill you can free the stone so that you are not punching against absolute resistance but against something that will free itself; you open it up like a Gruyère cheese before you cut it away. The drill technique was a very special mark of the Pisano school, but Giovanni used it as an expressive instrument as well as a practical one. He used it to give colour and texture to a surface so that if he wanted to make a beard have darkness, he would so drill it that it would take on a colour and a texture seen from a distance. This is one of the things that amazes me about him, this expressive use of the drill, not simply to make the job easier, but to accentuate its form. If you look at really primitive stone sculpture, such as early archaic Greek or Pre-Columbian work, you will find the drill used, but most of it is what we call 'rubbed sculpture', that's to say that after roughing out the forms with a punch, which breaks and stuns the stone, the craftsman got to work with abrasives, and rubbed the surface down until he got as far as he could beyond the stunning marks, and as smooth as he wanted his surface to be. By these means he got very simplified forms which are thought to be typically 'stone', but people think this because the sculptors did not have tools which could go beyond these simplicities; once you get a drilling technique as expert as Giovanni's you can go deeper into the stone and give it more expression, more colour, texture, light and shade.

But it's wrong to think that form and expression are separate things. For instance, if I put my hand on someone's shoulder, I can put it in a way that seems to be gripping or just gently touching. I may be touching it with affection and gentleness or I may be making some kind of empty gesture. All this is in the intention of the sculptor; it's part of his expression but it's part of form; you cannot separate the two. If you made a sculpture of Adam and Eve and Adam had his hand on Eve's shoulder, you could do it in a way that would show that he loved her or that he was ashamed of her; it's all done by a sensitivity to form, perhaps a greater sensitivity than is needed in dealing *only* with simple geometric abstract shapes – and it's in this way that Giovanni Pisano was a fully developed sculptor. His form, his abstraction, his sculptural qualities were integrated. The human and the abstract formal elements were inseparable and that is what I think really great sculpture should be.

The way Giovanni used and understood marble gave the stone life, the power to live from inside. Michelangelo said once 'the figure is in the stone; you have only to let it out', so that stone sculpture is not man-made but man-revealed. Giovanni let the inside of the stone come out; he freed something from the inside.

Giovanni Pisano's humanism has a quality which is for me the same as Rembrandt's humanism or Masaccio's humanism or the humanism of the late Michelangelo drawings. He was a man who showed in his sculpture the whole situation of the human being. It is, for me, this quality which makes Masaccio and Piero della Francesca and Rembrandt great. If I were asked to choose ten great artists, the greatest in European art, I would put Giovanni Pisano among them. It would be because of his understanding of life and of people. I feel terribly strongly that he was a great man because he understood human beings and if you asked me how I would judge great artists it would be on this basis. It would not be because they were clever in drawing or in carving or in painting or as designers;

something of these qualities they must naturally have, but their real greatness, to me, lies in their humanity.

These are the reasons why I wanted a book on Giovanni Pisano to be published. I wanted to convey by it something of the impact his sculpture had on me so that other people could see that they must go and look at that sculpture itself. I well remember going to Pisa one afternoon a few years ago to look once more at the Giovanni Pisanos and I was full of them that evening when I went to dinner with Walter and Eva Neurath at their house at Camaiore. What a shame it was, I said, that there was no book in English, so far as I knew, that gave Giovanni his due. Here was an artist who had done in sculpture things that Giotto and Masaccio would come to do in painting, but it was they who had got the credit for being the fathers of the Renaissance. I said that it seemed a pity that there was no book that tried to show what a great artist in sculpture Giovanni was.

'Why don't we do it?' Walter Neurath asked. 'Why doesn't Thames and Hudson do this? Would you help?'

I have helped as far as I could. I have spent many hours in Pisa and Siena with Michael Ayrton, who has shared my enthusiasm for twenty years and had proved it as long ago as that, by his lecture to the Royal Society of Arts from which his text has grown. Cavaliere Bessi, our photographer, was with us and I showed him in detail exactly what I wanted to bring out in the photographs. I wanted to illustrate that Giovanni Pisano approached the structure of sculpture from inside. Many early sculptors approached form from the outside, rounding it off and smoothing it, but Giovanni was one of the first Italians to feel the bone inside the sculpture and when we looked at the lions on the Pisa Cathedral pulpit and at the wolf in Siena, we could see how the elbow joints pushed out, that there was an inside structure, a skeleton to the sculpture coming out. It is not rubbed down, not sucked, like a sucked sweet, which is made unified because the outside is all smoothed. Looking at that lion and seeing that there were no smooth connections between the forms, I knew how Giovanni had understood the articulations of the figure. I would not easily nowadays give up time and energy to helping with a book, but I feel that in devoting both to this one I am doing something to repay a debt, for we are all indebted to Giovanni Pisano.

ACKNOWLEDGMENTS

My grateful thanks are due to Professor Ernst Gombrich for his help and encouragement, to Professor Joseph Rykwert for valuable comments and to Miss Barbara Steinberg for help in research. I am also grateful to Dr Max Seidel for permission to reproduce the head of 'Temperance' which he has identified as from the Tomb of Margaret of Luxembourg and to Dr Caterina Marcenaro for permission to publish the two other fragments which she discovered and which are parts of the same monument. No student of the period in sculpture with which this book is concerned, could fail to acknowledge Mr John Pope-Hennessy's invaluable publications on the subject and I am grateful that he was kind enough to read my work in typescript and to point out several errors of which I was guilty. Finally and above all my gratitude is due to my wife who, apart from continual help with the text, also aided me in the laborious activity of measuring every sculpture we studied together. M. A.

Acknowledgments are also due to the following for permission to reproduce the plates indicated: Anton Schroll Verlag, Vienna, 211, 214, 231; Archives Photographiques, Paris, f; Staatliche Museen, Berlin-Dahlem, 112, 167, 268, 302, 303, 304; Bildarchiv Foto Marburg, b, c; P and D. Colnaghi, 101; Mansell Collection, m, o, s, u, v, w, x, 12, 13, 110, 274, 276; The Metropolitan Museum of Art, New York, 287, 295, 296, 301; Henry Moore, 66; The Trustees of the National Gallery, London, t; Victoria and Albert Museum, London (Crown copyright), 114, 115, 212, 270.

Preface

THIS BOOK is intended to be the tribute paid by two sculptors to a great forerunner. Henry Moore is a born carver rather than a modeller and although much of his work is in bronze, stone and wood were his first chosen media. For myself I am a painter turned sculptor and painters, because they have a tendency to build up rather more than to cut away, are modellers. For this reason, wax and plaster which, worked direct, require both modelling and carving before being cast in bronze, have been my media. I am a metalworker and little if anything of Giovanni Pisano's work in metal remains. Nevertheless, sculpture is three-dimensional whatever its material. It exists and occupies space; its forms and their articulation in space are the essence of the art. Thus Moore, who taught me much about the essential nature of sculpture, and I, who was moved to practise it by Giovanni's overwhelming effect upon me, were brought together in this venture by our reverence for Giovanni's achievement. Our preliminary discussions took place at Forte dei Marmi, and it was there that he said for the first but not for the last time that 'we must prove that Giovanni Pisano was one of the greatest sculptors in the world, prove it to *people* – not art-historians, they know it – but people' – a distinction which few but the most firmly established artists would be wise to voice.

Fig. a   No town could be more appropriate than Forte dei Marmi to give birth to such a project. It lies below the quarries of Carrara from which Michelangelo obtained his marble and near those called San Giuliano which lie between Pisa and Lucca, from which Giovanni and his father Nicola obtained much of theirs. From his house below these mountains, Henry Moore goes daily to carve in marble every summer and it was at Pisa, a few miles away and a little over seven hundred years ago, that Giovanni Pisano began to make sculpture.

There is no standard work on Giovanni in English, nor is there any book in any language now in print which adequately illustrates his life-work. Both the volumes exclusively concerned with him are long out of print: Adolfo Venturi's pioneer study of 1928, although admirable, contains attributions which are no longer generally accepted, and Harald Keller's scholarly *Giovanni Pisano* was published in Vienna in 1942 in circumstances which precluded adequate photography and reproduction of the plates. For the rest, there are a large number of articles on Giovanni in learned journals and there are two substantial surveys in English, one of Italian Gothic sculpture and one of the whole period in Italian art to which he belonged. These discuss his sculpture at some length in its context.[1] *Notes on p. 201* There are also several books on Nicola Pisano[2] and there are separate volumes on those individual monuments such as the Siena Pulpit[3] and the Perugia Fountain[4] for which, in different degrees, both Nicola and Giovanni were responsible.

In terms of publication in book form, Nicola has so far come off rather better than his son, partly because he has been thought to stand at a clearer turning-point in Italian art-history and partly because he cannot so easily be filed away under the general term 'Gothic', which designation has done much to contain and something to obscure the true complexity of Giovanni's art. He receives high honour from art-historians, but the public does not view him, and never has, in the same 'proto-Renaissance' light as his father.

To many people interested in Italian art, the names of Giovanni's great contemporaries, Duccio and Giotto, are enough instantly to evoke an image of their art in the mind's eye. Not so in the case of Giovanni, whose name, however revered, conjures far less immediate a response from most people than those of the leading painters of his time. The reasons for this are, I think, several, and perhaps the fact that so little of Giovanni's sculpture has ever left the places for which it was carved is especially significant. The great museums of the world contain masterworks by Giotto, by Duccio and by Simone Martini, and since the advent of photographic reproduction their works have been almost as widely diffused in book form as the writings of their literary contemporaries Dante and Petrarch. Furthermore, important *trecento* paintings appear at intervals in the world's auction houses and fetch great prices, whereas the number of marbles by the great Pisan carvers to come upon the market are few indeed.

I believe that the only carvings by Giovanni Pisano to change hands during my adult life have been two fragments, from the tomb sculpture of Margaret of Luxembourg,[5] and the upper half of a full-length figure, from the façade of Siena Cathedral, representing the prophet Haggai which was acquired for the Victoria and Albert Museum in London by the present director Mr John Pope-Hennessy, who was also responsible for the discovery in the same museum of a small ivory carving of Christ Crucified which he convincingly attributes to Giovanni and which had gone unrecognized since its acquisition in 1867 for the sum of £15. That two of Giovanni's carvings may be listed as being in the Victoria and Albert Museum due to Mr Pope-Hennessy's scholarship and his astonishing eye is the more remarkable when it is realized that there are so few others outside Italy. A crucifix carved in boxwood and a marble lectern from the Pisa pulpit are in the Berlin Museum, while four further fragments from the same pulpit by Giovanni are in the Metropolitan Museum, New York.[6] All other known sculptures generally accepted as by Giovanni Pisano remain at least in the cities for which he made them, if not always where he intended them to be in those cities.

His major works are at Pisa, Siena and Pistoia, but the serious student must also visit Genoa, Padua, Perugia and Prato, a modest enough itinerary for any visitor who might wish to make for himself the last great personal discovery of an unfamiliar Italian sculptor of towering genius which remains to be made.

The didactic and evangelical urge which compels people, whether well- or ill-equipped to do so, to celebrate splendours which they feel should be more widely shared is one ingrained in me. I can never resist it and I am well aware of the dangers I risk in the highly specialized field of scholarship upon which I here trespass. On the other hand, Henry Moore has shown no such compulsion during his long, productive and wisely spent life. He has spoken, from time to time in public, of what he most admires; he has never before, to my knowledge, wished so strongly to celebrate a forerunner's achievement as to collaborate upon a book of this kind.

As to the adequacy of the text as a work of scholarship, I must seek to turn aside the wrath of those with a larger competence, and this I do by invoking T.S. Eliot, who says in the preface to his pamphlet on Dante that 'a contemporary writer of verse' should be required 'only to give a faithful account of his acquaintance with the poet of whom he writes'. Thus I, as a contemporary maker of sculptures, feel I may follow this example and treat of my acquaintance with Giovanni Pisano as a sculptor rather than as an architect, also avoiding, as far as possible, lengthy participation in the vexed controversies whereby established scholars prove themselves, as to the exact distribution of hands, the degree to which a given marble is the product of the master alone or was carved with assistance from his workshop, and whence exactly he drew his sources of style; on these and other important but recondite matters I can only venture personal and tentative views. Learned opinions on such matters sometimes reflect profound studies in iconography, sometimes the natural chauvinism of those who claim Giovanni to be wholly dependent upon Italian sources of inspiration, and sometimes the cosmopolitanism of others who have pointed out his debt to France.[7] Sometimes such opinions reveal those whose belief in their own *style-critique* is so profound as to make them suppose their judgement to be wholly objective. In my opinion, the solution to a sculptural problem leads the sculptor to use any source or any device of which he becomes aware, and it seems likely that a Pisan, at the latter end of the thirteenth century, would have been well aware of what was going on elsewhere. He would have had access to numerous sources of the schemata and minutiae of his trade whether he himself travelled to see them or they, in one form or another, came to be shown to him.

Furthermore, he lived in an age of spiritual stress and physical turbulence,[8] which I believe to be reflected in his sculpture, and since I am unconvinced by the frequently accepted fancy that artists live wholly remote from the political, social and theological problems of the times to which they belong, I probably trespass upon my 'acquaintance with' the sculptor of whom I write, to extrapolate beyond the bounds of securely established evidence.

A man loves where he can identify and to me the moment in 1947 when I first saw, at the Museo San Matteo at Pisa, the great exhibition which set the full range of early Tuscan sculpture before my startled eyes so shook me, so added to my mind a new dimension, so altered my life, that this celebration twenty years later I regard as a *devoir* to a sculptor of whom I then knew nothing, decently educated in the visual arts though I vaingloriously thought myself to be. To me, the great half-length figures in high relief, taken down from the façade of the Pisa Baptistry, so eroded by exposure to the elements as to seem stripped of all corporeal detail, stood forth in a grandeur so overwhelming   *Pls 64–79* that they seemed to me the frozen essence of spiritual power. In the utter silence which great sculpture of its nature can impose upon the mind while its forms speak, it was as if each worn figure had, like Lear, suffered to voice the storm and drowned a tempest seven hundred years prolonged.

Moore has said that other figures, worked more fully 'in the round', from the façade of the same Baptistry and now in the Pisa Museum first captured him as long ago as 1925. He is more moved   *Pls 85–91* by Giovanni's capacity to 'release action by freeing the figure from the stone', as he puts it, than by the complex and high drama, the exposition of archetypes, or by profound narrative; in my passion for these, as a practising sculptor, I do not seem to be a child of my time. Yet we have both been changed by our cognisance of the sculpture of Giovanni Pisano and both of us share a reverence and a passion for his art. Therefore we celebrate it in this book.

a. The quarry of S. Guiliano, near Pisa

b

c

d

e

f

g

1 The Gothic Frame

b. The Visitation. c 1220. Reims Cathedral. Right wall of the central portal of the West Front

c. Madonna. Trumeau figure. Late 13th century. North Portal, Notre Dame de Paris

d. GUIDO DA COMO. Pulpit. Church of S. Bartolommeo, Pisa

e. *Atalante*. c 1220. Musée de l'Œuvre Notre Dame, Strasbourg

f. Head of Christ. Reims Cathedral, West Front. Musée Lapidaire, Paris

g. Unfinished relief of the Nativity by a follower of Giovanni Pisano. Museo di S. Matteo, Pisa

THE TERM 'Gothic' with which Giovanni has long been labelled invokes a mental image which is both valid and misleading. The Gothic style was a northern invention and however profoundly Giovanni was subject to its influence, he was an Italian and equally, if not more, susceptible to his native sources and to the lingering and never wholly severed tradition of Italy's classical past. The Gothic style moved southwards during the twelfth and thirteenth centuries, replacing or modifying the Romanesque, combining with the neo-classicism fostered by the Emperor Frederick II in southern Italy, penetrating *la maniera greca* from Byzantium and eclipsing the remnants of the Carolingian, to create an amalgam which has been pigeonholed as 'Italian Gothic'. It is a pigeonhole richly furnished with crockets and finials, with tracery and pointed arches, and it is as large as a cathedral but it is atypical, even peripheral, to the North Alpine mainstream. Furthermore it neither wholly contains Giovanni nor has it housed him to the advantage of his reputation. Even during his lifetime opposition was forming in central Italy towards the foreign cultural invasion from the north which the Gothic was seen to be. Nor was it solely cultural; it was also political. The subjection of the papacy to political pressure and especially to the hegemony of the Angevin dynasty, following the demise of the Hohenstaufen empire, played their part in stirring an Italian reaction which was to increase during subsequent centuries when Italy took the centre of the stage in the visual arts.

The term Gothic was initially applied to architecture, embracing only by implication those sister arts of painting and sculpture whose forms were determined by their architectural setting. Thus the pejorative criticism which the Gothic received from early writers on the subject was directed towards forms in building rather than towards those in sculpture and painting. We see the Gothic now as an integration of all the visual arts within a dominant style with specific characteristics but in Italy a certain paradox existed which caused the critics of a 'barbarian' and foreign architectural invasion to celebrate the very painters who were subject to it, hailing them separately as innovators.

The opposition to the Gothic was gradually intensified as the nostalgia for the ancient world increased. The idea that art was being 'reborn' in the work of Giotto and Cimabue gained ground when Boccaccio, taking his lead from Dante, singled out these masters. He was among the first to conceive, in proto-Renaissance humanist terms, of such a re-birth. Villani, too, regarded Cimabue as 'having revived the bloodless, almost extinct art' of painting. Despite the fact that in both painting and sculpture the entire fourteenth century was dominated by, or at least submitted in large measure to, the hegemony of the 'barbarism' from the north, few had a good word to say for it and after Ghiberti it was not only disapproved but gradually superseded, a process which took considerably longer than those who disapproved may have wished. Indeed the disapprobation of Gothic architecture only reaches its climax in the sixteenth century.

Filarete, writing in 1464, shrewdly condemned it as having flooded Italy with 'customs and traditions from north of the Alps (proceeding) not from real architects but from painters, stone-masons and in particular goldsmiths who practised what they liked and understood', so that 'great buildings came to be fashioned in the likeness of tabernacles and censers'. It is also condemned in a *Life of Brunelleschi* probably written by the mathematician Manetti in the 1480's, while in the famous letter to Pope Leo X, attributed to Baldassare Castiglione and Raphael, the Gothic was defined as the act of barbarians who built in terms of 'living trees, their branches bent and joined at the top'.[1]   *Notes on p. 201*

Our view of the Middle Ages still tends to be swayed by a vestigially Pre-Raphaelite notion, in which we are tempted to see, in the raising of the great northern cathedrals, the symbols of a golden age of faith in which Gothic masterpieces were produced under the supervision of piously anonymous masters of architecture, sculpture, painting, illumination and all allied crafts. We picture numerous workshops combining to create and to fill splendid buildings with treasure by virtue of the collective endeavour of simple craftsmen under the enlightened patronage of such great and learned men as the Abbot Suger of St Denis. As with many such golden generalizations, this one is not without its truths, and the story of the raising of Chartres after the fire of 1194 is a proof of it. On the other hand, it is improbable that other master-masons and great sculptors were either more remarkable for modesty or more humbly desirous of anonymity than Gislebertus of Autun who firmly signed his tympanum, below the feet of his carved Christ in majesty, or Wiligelmo who made no bones as to his own excellence in his inscription on the façade of the Cathedral of Modena. It is true that the style of St Denis, in that it could almost be called Suger's invention, has caused his name to be preserved where those of his craftsmen are lost, but the phase of anonymity among the masters was short-lived.

Undoubtedly the status of the 'mechanical' arts, which included painting, sculpture and architecture, had always remained below that of the 'liberal' arts. The tradition of this inferiority had been established in the ancient world, as Plutarch showed, while Seneca, whose influence on medieval thought was profound, had gone out of his way to remark that painting and sculpture were manual rather than intellectual activities. Added to this, the long-remembered teachings of Gregory the Great who, in the 6th century AD, declared that painting and church ornament were valuable in churches for those who could not read and 'carried with them', as Larner puts it, 'the implication that art itself was an activity particularly appropriate for the understanding of the uneducated and for the minds of the illiterate.' Being thus 'mechanical' the artist was by implication 'a mere hand, subordinate to the directing mind of the priest-patron'.[2] But given that these beliefs were widely held, it is impossibly difficult to know how much they truly applied; certainly the mould in which the sculptor or painter, as a 'base mechanical', had been cast was at breaking-point by the end of the thirteenth century. Furthermore, it was in Italy and with Giovanni and Giotto that this stereotype was finally broken, if it ever wholly applied to the masters as opposed to their artisans. Although Nicola Pisano had firmly established himself by 1260 as an individual held in high regard, it was his son Giovanni who first added to his own signature an inscription which, by virtue of its remarkable frankness, constitutes the first fragment of 'autobiography' by a medieval sculptor to have been preserved to us. It is something of a paradox that he, who emerges more clearly in the light of day as a human being than his father, should today be less familiar as a name to the public at large. Nor does the paradox cease there. Nicola's fame has partly rested upon a classicism stemming from antique derivations, a classicism such as had flour-

Fig. b ished at Reims a generation earlier; while the Gothic style for which Giovanni is famed was first introduced into Italian sculpture by Nicola.

Nicola was both classic and Gothic; his son was both Gothic and classic and it is largely because the terms carry such weight and the word *Gothic* defines in Panofsky's heavy-laden term a 'mega-period',[3] that Giovanni's reputation is weighed down with a far from precise designation which would come to be overshadowed by the 'reborn' classicism of the Renaissance a century after his death, whereas Nicola at least came to be given high commendation as a forerunner of this rebirth.

Medieval man had not been concerned with aesthetic 'rebirth' nor with an emergence from 'dark ages'. That notion arises in the fourteenth century.[4] The medieval craftsman's relationship with the classical past was in many ways more relaxed, being less self-conscious, than that of the Renaissance in that he wove such remains of the Roman and Greek worlds as were available to him into his existing schemata by making pagan images perform Christian functions, so that an Eros became *Amor carnalis*, a Sisyphus could stand for Pride and a Hercules could stand for Samson no less than for Fortitude. As Panofsky also points out, 'the acme of medieval classicism was reached within the general framework of the Gothic style' and they were not divided. By contrast Renaissance man, believing himself to have stepped into the light after a long night, established the classical past as something from which he had been barbarously separated and cut off. He re-established this lost Utopia at a fixed point in time and looked back towards it seeking a return to a golden age, whereas medieval man had regarded it as still alive and capable of incorporation into the arts providing it had been properly embraced by the Christian faith.

It is a measure of the unjustly distributed weight of 'megaperiods' that Nicola and Giovanni should continue to be regarded as inextricably set in the medieval matrix, whether classic or Gothic-classic, whereas Giotto, who was Giovanni's contemporary, suffers no such relentless categorizing. All three shared a climate of ideas; Giotto's debt to the Pisani was real enough, and he did less to free the figure from its architectural straitjacket than did Giovanni; but Giotto escaped Renaissance censure in no small degree as a result of a favourable mention from Dante and avoided the stigma of Gothicism even if in fact the *zeitgeist* was as powerful in his age as in any other.

The irony here involved is poignant, since Dante in the eleventh canto of the *Purgatorio* remarked Giotto's status whilst castigating another painter, Oderisi da Gubbio, for the sin of pride, and referred sadly to the temporary nature of fame: with regard to Cimabue: *Credetto Cimabue nella pittura/ tener lo campo ed ora ha Giotto il grido / si che la fama di colui è oscura.* (Cimabue thought to hold the field in painting and now Giotto has the cry, so that the fame of the other is obscured.) Having secured the *grido*, Giotto held it firmly and has done so ever since, becoming to all intents and purposes the first truly 'famous artist' since antiquity.

This kind of fortuitous historical circumstance has played its part in the making of great reputations, but another factor also plays a part and that is the hold which painting has taken on public taste during the centuries since Giotto. Despite Donatello, despite Michelangelo and the few other mountain peaks of sculpture which tower over the landscape of the visual arts, it has been painting and not sculpture which has been pre-eminent in the public eye since the Middle Ages and much that occurred in sculpture in Giotto's time has come to be treated as subordinate to the great advance made in the illusion of plasticity he gave to pictorial form. Yet sculpture played then, and continued to play, a decisive role in the evolution of this very illusion of plasticity. In the following century Masaccio demonstrated it, Leon Battista Alberti made it dogma and when, later, Vasari came to write of Giovanni Pisano as a precursor of the Renaissance, his regard for Giovanni, as for Giotto, was based on their seminal role as creators of solid beings occupying either actual or convincingly illusory deep space. This adds a further paradox to the confusion, for the Gothic style in painting is generally visualized as a linear convention which accommodates the figure in the shallow symbolic depth imposed by the gold ground, whereas much Gothic figure sculpture hides below massive canopies and in deep niches which encompass and contain it. That this convention obtained well into the fifteenth century may be seen in the sculpture on the façade of Or San Michele in Florence.

In contrast to these conventions Giovanni perched his free-standing figures upon the façade of Siena Cathedral, where they crane out into space as if to demonstrate their lack of dependence upon their setting. They establish more powerfully perhaps than any other carvings of their period 'the principle of axiality', further to quote Panofsky, which prevailed in sculpture from Greece in the fifth century BC until the collapse of the Greco-Roman world. This principle, reintroduced by Gothic sculptors, proposes that 'a form projecting from a plane outside itself be conceived as centred around an axis within itself'. It is essential to the independence of the gesture made by any figure portrayed in action as sculpture in the round. It is equally important in the portrayal of a figure in painting conceived as an illusion of a solid, occupying illusory space in depth. In order fully to act upon this principle, a painted figure must be given such deep space to act within and a sculptured figure must move out from the niche.[5]

In the sculptured relief, the provision of a spacious arena for action would be required to wait for Ghiberti's second set of bronze doors for the Florentine Baptistry. There he would take from painting the means to create the illusion, using Brunelleschi's perspective system to give a wide acting area to his protagonists, but the restless energy of the *dramatis personae* on the crowded panels of Giovanni's pulpit reliefs and their impatience of restriction ordained the necessity. Despite the freedom he gave them in the height of their relief, they often seem to demand even more real space, in which to act, than he could give them.

The dialogue between sculpture and painting which emanated from Tuscany at the turn of the fourteenth century was one from which both the arts of painting and sculpture drew benefit. Giotto and Giovanni share a plastic idiom which is distinct from that of Simone Martini and the elegant masters of arabesque who followed him. In Siena only the Lorenzetti among painters were truly a party to this visual discussion as to the nature of space and the room to move in it. In this context, it is of passing interest that Pietro Lorenzetti became guardian of the children of Tino di Camaino, Giovanni's most famous pupil, after Tino's death. Children may be observed to occupy a great deal of space.

Despite the lead suggested by Giotto, the illusion of space in depth played little part in fourteenth-century painting, whilst in relief carving it was taken no further than Giovanni took it. It was a century later that the implications of Giotto's advance came to be understood, and with them Giovanni's. Thus when Masaccio was working, with Donatello as his neighbour, upon the polyptich for the Church of the Carmine at Pisa, which he completed in 1426, he must daily have seen the masterpieces of Nicola and Giovanni and the sculptural solutions which they had achieved to the problem of relating bulky solids within a Gothic framework. Masaccio's commission was to paint a polyptich within the Gothic convention on a gold ground, a convention which he must have found tiresomely archaic since he had already evolved the illusion of deep space in which his weighty figures needed *Fig. t* to have their being. The resulting compromise in which Masaccio's Madonna seems to press the gold ground back, as if it were an uncomfortable restriction rather than a symbol of infinity, exactly echoes, more than a century after Giovanni's death, the sense of restriction to which his relief carving seems subject on the panels of his pulpits. Thus both at the opening and closing of the central Gothic century in Italy a similar lack of ease prevails. Two giants strive to reject their niches.

No one questions Masaccio's debt to Giotto. It is only just to suggest that Giovanni also contributed something of great importance to Masaccio's short, tremendous life.

Because the history of art in Italy after Giotto comes to tower over all Western Europe, it is all too readily supposed that Italy has always stood central in the mainstream. In fact when, during the second quarter of the thirteenth century, the Gothic tide from the north, predominantly from the Domaine Royale and Champagne, poured into Italy, her arts were by no means flourishing. In terms of Europe, Italy was provincial. The cathedrals of Reims and Amiens, the abbey of Westminster and those parts of the fabric of Chartres erected after the fire of 1194, were built by the mid-thirteenth century, and the majority of the greatest Gothic ecclesiastical structures in the north were either built or planned by the time Nicola Pisano's first pulpit was completed at Pisa in 1260. The southern flooding of this tide owed much to the architects of the Cistercian Order, whose northern influence even penetrated such neo-classical Imperial monuments as the Capuan Gate set up by the Emperor Frederick in Apulia.

Northern Italy especially, at this period, was still dominated by the Romanesque and by *la maniera greca*, or provincial Byzantinism. It was subject to pressure from *la maniera moderna*, the 'barbarian' Gothic, yet it clung tenaciously to *la maniera antica*, its classic past, and it is a measure of the confusion of these terms that Vasari later came to use *la maniera antica greca* to mean classical and *la maniera moderna* to mean not Gothic but 'modern' or Renaissance.

The prevalence of *la maniera greca* together with *la maniera antica* at Pisa is not surprising. One of the great centres of maritime power, in regular contact with Byzantium, she had created her great Romanesque ecclesiastical complex in the twelfth century, and disposed about the city a substantial number of Roman sarcophagi and other fragments of antique carving, taken in war, imported or excavated. Furthermore, there is every reason to suppose that small Greek and Etruscan bronzes, ancient coins and carved gems lay in private hands. How these conflicting styles, together with the invasion of the Gothic, merged into the art of the Pisani is a matter of some debate. My own instincts tend to advance the classical past as the most potent element to sway the balance, but the weight of the Gothic *maniera moderna* was not to be ignored. As Pope-Hennessy puts it, 'There persisted in the greater part of the peninsula a classical tradition far more pervasive and more strongly rooted than in the North. In medieval France the sculptural relics of the Roman occupation exercised an intermittent influence on style and, especially at Reims, classical forms were absorbed into the tissue of Gothic art. In Italy, on the other hand, the antique existed as a force in its own right, at first resisting and then tempering the new style which filtered southwards from beyond the Alps. For this reason Gothic in Italy evolved not as a dialect of French Gothic, but as an independent language with a syntax, grammar and vocabulary of its own.'[6]

This sculptural language was first spoken clearly by Nicola Pisano in his pulpit for the Pisa Baptistry. It was a language fully formed when we first hear his voice in marble. His son spoke it and so did Arnolfo di Cambio, Nicola's great follower, each in a different accent. Far from having their individual identities submerged, each established himself as an individual and of the three it is Giovanni who emerges most clearly as a man. Despite the paucity of documents, the whole romantically conceived picture of a simple and pious master-mason, content to work submissively at his calling, collapses in the presence of Giovanni's fierce individuality and restless spirit. He was a man possessed, sharing, as no other forerunner has, the desperation of Michelangelo. He was one of those very rare artists who could rise to equal a father of such a comparable genius. It may be fanciful to see him as uncomfortably bearing the weight of Nicola's greatness upon his shoulders but it is not impossible that he felt that weight.

2 Nicola Pisano and the Climate of his Time

Nicola Pisano – and it is essential that the father should introduce the son – was born during the first decades of the thirteenth century, perhaps as early as 1210. It seems highly probable that he came from Apulia in Southern Italy, since he is twice referred to in Sienese documents as 'de Apulia' rather than 'de Pisis'. It is also likely that his classicism derived initially from contact with sculptors employed to further the Emperor Frederick's strenuous efforts to promote a local classical 'Renaissance' of his own.

The first carvings traditionally associated with Nicola are some small corbel figures in a tower of the Emperor's Castel del Monte, although these are of little merit and could be the work of any of Frederick's host of masons. He may have worked under Nicolo di Bartolommeo da Foggia at Ravello and elsewhere in the Campania, but he is first known to be in Tuscany in 1258, when his name figures in a will drawn up at Lucca. How long he had been at Pisa before he began his pulpit for the Baptistry is unknown, but he must certainly have been an established master to have been awarded so costly and important a commission. The pulpit is signed and dated 1260. It is a landmark in the history of Italian sculpture, an extraordinary departure from precedent bearing as little resemblance to such pulpits as that of Guglielmo, now at Cagliari, or that of Guido da Como at Pistoia *Fig. d* – which antedates Nicola's by only ten years – as a Picasso of 1910 bears to a Pissarro of 1900.

Guido's pulpit in S. Bartolommeo in Pantano in Pistoia is a severe Lombard-Romanesque work. It shows scenes from the life of Christ in five panels, each of which is laterally divided into two. The angle statuettes show the evangelists with their symbols and the whole rectangular structure is supported against the wall of the church by three columns, two of which stand on lions and one upon the back of a crouched male figure. The sculpture has virtues but it is to Nicola's pulpit what Kyd's version of *Hamlet* is to Shakespeare's.

Fig. k   Nicola's great freestanding polygonal structure with its archivolt formed by decorated trilobate arches, its seven supporting columns, and above all its majestically conceived panels portraying the Annunciation, the Nativity, the Adoration of the Magi, the Presentation in the Temple, the Crucifixion and the Last Judgement – each carved with a depth of undercut and a complexity of composition wholly in advance of any Italian work of art of its time – also contains a body of imagery unprecedented in the pulpits of the period. In its sophistication, as imagery to be 'read' while the priest spoke or read to the congregation, it was incomparable, not only as sculpture but for the body of visual information which it contains. This ordering of factual and symbolic information must presuppose either a learned Scholastic 'programme' or a high degree of Scholastic learning on the part of Nicola

Notes on p. 201   himself,[1] for no sculptural concept of its time better illustrates St Thomas Aquinas' precept *nam et sensus ratio quaedam est* (for the sense, too, is a kind of reason), and like the Saint's great *Summa Theologica* the pulpit aims at an intellectual totality by a perfectly related arrangement of parts and parts of parts.

I fully recognize the danger in making even a metaphorical comparison between the *Summa* and the programming of the Pisani pulpits. Obviously the abstruse arguments as to philosophical positions contained in the *Summa* could not begin to be mirrored in stone carving. Nevertheless the potency of philosophical ideas as to the nature of reality may not have been wholly irrelevant to a sculptor whose art was dedicated to the creation of a physical world in little; to a reality couched in metaphor at a time when rising debate centred upon what might be considered real in the physical world.

The pulpits were intended to be works of instruction and the exposition they were designed to illuminate was very far from simple. To view them merely as harmoniously composed art objects is to impoverish them. To the sophisticated, the visual narrative was required to supply as many levels of communication as the poetic, each operating distinctly and yet dependent upon each other for the enrichment of the whole. In *The Divine Comedy*, as Dante was at pains to describe it to Can Grande della Scala,[2] there were six matters which must be inquired into at the beginning, 'to wit the *subject, agent, form* and *end, the title of the work* and *the branch* of philosophy it concerns'. He chose three of them to expand upon at length, pointing out that 'the sense of this work is not simple but on the contrary polysemous, that is to say "of more senses than one".'

Thus, in the programme of a major work of narrative sculpture, levels comparable to those desirable in poetry were as necessary as in any written 'work of instruction' (for so Dante termed his poem). The literal, the allegorical, the philosophic, the anagogic, the typological and the tropological (or moral) instruction to be conveyed, all needed to be 'inquired into' by the spectator and all were elaborate. For instance, the Four Evangelists as images also symbolized not only the Four Rivers of

Paradise but the Four Elements;[3] these in turn 'flowed' from a polygonal shape in Nicola's pulpit which manifested a symbolic geometry of great antiquity. The earth was symbolically conceived as a square, a quadrilateral form which embraced the four elements, the four points of the compass, and the four seasons together with four paradisal rivers, the Geon, the Pison, the Tigris and the Euphrates, which flowed to the corners. The square of the earth may be geometrically if imperfectly related to the circle as the symbol representing heaven (self-enclosed and without angles, since God has neither beginning nor end) by 'squaring the circle', an insoluble geometrical problem which had obsessed mathematicians for many centuries. The nearest practical resolution of this problem is the polygon which, although it can only be an approximation, creates a union of both symbols.

Apart from its geometrical form, the faces of the polygon were numerically significant, the hexagon representing the death of Christ on the sixth day of the week extended in the octagon to embrace His Resurrection. The *Fons Vitae*, like the Fountain of Paradise in medieval imagery, is frequently polygonal and as early as 423–440 the Lateran Baptistry was changed from a circular to an octagonal structure. This octagonal plan became fairly usual thereafter and those of Florence and Pistoia are characteristic of Tuscan examples. Parma Baptistry, on the other hand, which was begun in 1196, has an octagonal exterior containing a circular baptismal chamber. At Pisa, the Baptistry begun by Diotisalvi in 1152 is circular, symbolically representing rebirth into the family of the Church, whereas the font by Guido Bigarelli is an octagon. It was presumably to reinforce the metaphor that Nicola constructed his pulpit as a hexagon, creating within a Baptistry, which contains a sacramental fountain of rebirth in Christ, a structure which signifies a fountain of discourse audible during the span of human life from birth to death.

The idea that mathematics and geometry in particular were a divine activity by which God had planned and structured the universe, goes back to Pythagoras. Plato, in the *Timaeus*, presented the god as 'always doing geometry'. It was transmitted circuitously but none the less potently to the medieval mind, where, since the squaring of the circle was (as it remains) the most intractable problem in Euclidean geometry, it sorted well with the striving for architectonic 'perfection'.

Nicola did not invent the polygonal pulpit; there are earlier examples in Tuscany and in the south, notably at Moscufo, but he achieved its apogee in the Pisa Baptistry at a time when the practice of building baptistries detached from the main structure of the church itself would shortly cease. The main reason for this was the virtual cessation of adult baptisms. As J. G. Davies puts it: 'The preponderance of candidates for baptism in a country normally Christian will inevitably be infants... This means that on the one hand, large fonts were no longer necessary and, on the other hand, that separate buildings in which the nude adults could be baptised in a seemly fashion of semi-privacy were redundant.'[4]

It is significant, however, that the first great polygonal sculptured pulpit in European art should have been erected in a baptistry and that the succeeding pulpits by Nicola and his son should also have been polygonal. In Giovanni's octagonal pulpit for Pisa Cathedral not only is the circle so nearly squared that optically its eight carved panels give the structure the appearance of being circular, but its two additional straight panels which are set to protrude from an empty face of the octagon suggest in miniature the form of the ambulatory so common to baptistries of an earlier period.

At the philosophical level the complex neo-Platonism of the time which had been filtered through Hellenistic, Islamic and Hebrew writings was in some degree of contest with Aristotelianism, which further complicated the significant meaning of concepts to be portrayed. So involuted were the strands of theological, philosophical and 'historical' instruction involved in exposition, where history could be construed to concern salvation, that presumably only the few could fully comprehend these abstruse matters. It was these few sophisticates who must have been called upon to instruct the sculptors and painters and in turn to derive the most profound intellectual, spiritual and aesthetic satisfaction from the results, but it would be wrong to assume that the many were wholly ignorant. All were concerned *to know*, as much as each individual was capable of knowing, for salvation lay at the end of the path and all held the elements of Christian narrative and symbolism in common. Everyone would have striven, within the limits of his capacity, to 'read' the full burden of the instruction intended.

The physical world, however, appears disorderly unless it is seen and understood as divinely ordered, despite appearances. It was and has remained the task of the artist to reveal in little the pattern of this order just as it is among the duties of the priest to convince mankind of its immutability. Thus a sculptured pulpit must make this order palpably and visibly explicit in symbolic form. No exposition could be more consequential, for the pulpit girded the priest with the tangible and visible sign of the intellectual and spiritual sources of his discourse. And that discourse was most notably broadened and extended at the time when Nicola and Giovanni were at work.

Until Urban IV and his successors drastically reduced the power of the diocesan bishops in order to concentrate power centrally in the Curia, bishops alone had preached.[5] It was the papal privilege extended to the Mendicant Orders to preach both in Latin and in the vernacular, in all places, with or without the permission of the bishop, that so profoundly and dramatically increased the importance of the pulpit. The members of the Mendicant Orders not only preached, but they disagreed sharply on many points of doctrine and in airing their differences from the pulpit they altered the relationship between the clergy and the laity once and for all.

The divergences of opinion between the two greatest preaching orders, the Dominican and the Franciscan, were a burning issue. The touchstone of Dominican theology was Aquinas' *Summa* with its central tenet of clearly expressed reason in logical exposition. The Franciscans, on the other hand, took from their founder the teaching of a more subjective and a more flexible doctrine, the force of which lay in St Francis' apostolic idealism and his attestedly immediate experience of God.

It was the pattern of Dominican thought which instigated the clarity, order and classical concern with natural appearances of Nicola's pulpit, but since tides ebb and flow in thought as they do in nature, the synthetic power of reason did not prove the whole answer to human aspiration. The need was also for direct experience of God. Thus in the formative years of Giovanni Pisano, deeply conflicting views must have been delivered from, among many others, the very pulpits created by Nicola and his son. Nor were these issues limited to cut-and-dried theological postulates.

There existed a spectrum of opinion in terms of the precise interpretation of doctrine in each order and much political and social opposition between the friars and the faculties and as the Mendicants extended their teaching activities to penetrate the universities, an increasing conflict with the secular clergy, who had come to be regarded as wholly corrupt.[6]

It was, therefore, in a time of intense theological and philosophical controversy that Giovanni Pisano was born. The controversy was to continue throughout his lifetime.

Nicola created his Baptistry pulpit in the decade of Pisa's last momentous triumph and on the brink of her decline,[7] which can be seen in retrospect as dating from the death of the Emperor Frederick in 1250.

Pisa had two centuries of prosperity behind her. She had great timber forests from which she built her navy and her trading vessels and in these vessels she exported furs, leather, wool, iron and salt in great quantity. She controlled the marble quarries of Carrara and served as the port for the export of marble. It is not therefore surprising that the great complex of ecclesiastical architecture she raised to celebrate her prosperity during the twelfth century should have drawn architects and sculptors to her gates. Nor is it remarkable that, during the thirteenth century, Pisa produced the greatest sculpture and the greatest sculptors in marble in all Italy. All the ingredients were available, including a guild of metal workers famous throughout the land. Having brought sculptors to her, she bred from them. From the north, down the Via Francigena – a road the possession of which was continually disputed by Lucca – came trade from France and elsewhere and by this route, also, came the merchants and craftsmen who brought the Gothic style to Italy. Other men and materials came by sea from both north and east and by land and sea from the south. The treasures of two Empires, together with their fabricators, found their way to Pisa.

Merchants from both north and east brought saleable artefacts in different styles and executed by different methods and these would have been studied and would have stimulated Pisan craftsmen. What they must also have brought, which is less often remarked, were tools which would come to affect the techniques of marble carving. New steels and methods of tempering came out of Syria during the first half of the thirteenth century. Even more important, new smelting techniques had been evolved in Germany.[8] A now forgotten 'industrial revolution' had occurred which would eventually enable Michelangelo to cut obliquely into the marble block and accurately to fetch away slivers of it a finger's length long, in a fashion which since late Hellenistic and Roman times had been technically impractical. Michelangelo's sculpture was made possible in no small measure because, three centuries earlier, during the reign of the Emperor Frederick, chisels hard and sharp enough to make practical so drastic an attack on marble had again begun to be forged.

The factors which gave rise to these improvements are several. Iron production throughout Europe began to rise in the twelfth century and continued to increase for three hundred years thereafter. The Catalan forge, the medieval equivalent of the blast furnace, came into being. It was followed by the *Stuchofen* developed early in the fourteenth century in the Harz region of western Germany. Iron smelting and forging, despite such curious suppositions as that 'tools are given harder tempering in the urine of a small redheaded boy than in ordinary water', became remarkably proficient and perhaps further innovations came from Damascus, the source of the best wrought iron and steel in the medieval world. The Damascus blade is famous in the history of weapons. It required a highly skilled and specialized forging technique. To what extent the skills employed by the swordsmith directly affected the manufacture of the lowly chisel is highly speculative, but it would be remarkable if they did not, and Damascus steel acquired either from the Empire in the South through its close association with the Muslim world, or from the Empire of the East in trade, must have become available.

De Rerum Proprietatibus, an encyclopaedia containing considerable information on metallurgy by Bartolomeus Anglicus, a Franciscan friar writing in 1250, was known throughout Italy within the following thirty years. It would be strange if the Pisans were not among the first to have acquired it, since their armourers had been famous as early as 1228, when they were invited south to work for the Emperor. But this does not mean that a lesser master than Giovanni would have had the courage and resource to employ so revolutionary a tool as a chisel which could cut into stone so readily and so irrevocably.

It is very difficult to gauge the extent to which the flat chisel was generally employed. An *Fig. 9* unfinished relief by a follower of Giovanni at Pisa,[9] which makes use of motifs from both the Nativity of the Baptist and the Nativity panel of Giovanni's Pisa pulpit, could not conceivably have been advanced in depth and undercut to the level of Giovanni's examples. This unfinished relief is only advanced to its present condition by means of the most tentative use of the flat chisel as a finishing tool. Apart from this, it is a carving produced by exactly the same methods as those used in the fifth-century BC pediment sculptures at Olympia, as opposed to the later Hellenistic and Roman additions to those sculptures, upon which the flat chisel was extensively employed. This argues that Giovanni's imitator viewed the flat chisel with no great confidence, whereas there is every sign that Giovanni *Pl. 140* had used it with absolute mastery in the Massacre of the Innocents panel of the Pistoia pulpit, if not before.

The antique method of shaping the stone with the punch had the advantage, however laborious, of keeping the whole work safely in progress at the same degree of completion throughout every stage prior to the finish, and this the archaic Greeks, lacking a tool which would maintain its edge, achieved with the rubbing stone. The Hellenistic Greeks, and subsequently the Romans, could temper chisels which could cut marble without stunning it, as the surface of the so-called Praxitelean Hermes proves. At some period after the fall of the Roman Empire, these metallurgical techniques were lost, to be rediscovered in the thirteenth century. But tools so sharp that one disastrous chisel stroke could ruin a whole work may well have deterred the uncertain or conservative craftsman.

Keller[10] states that the flat chisel was not used in Florentine workshops before 1294 and did not reach Orvieto[11] until 1310. This suggests that the development of new tools and the improvement of old ones was the gradual process that it might be expected to be. It would be perfectly comprehensible if the full possibilities of the flat chisel remained a closely guarded professional secret in Pisa for a decade or more, since it was not the shape of the blade which was the determining factor but its tempering and its handling.

Upon the quality of the tools available the choice of stone obviously depended. The marble of San Giuliano was easier to work, but unfortunately this very fact made it more easily susceptible to weather. No external monumental sculptures by either Nicola or Giovanni are made from the hard, dense marble of Carrara. All those which ornamented the façade of the Pisa Baptistry were made from the more porous and friable stone of San Giuliano, whereas the marbles of the Siena pulpit were contractually stipulated to be from Carrara. The marble from which Giovanni's monumental sculptures for the façade of Siena Cathedral were carved has proved permeable, for they are sadly eroded. On the other hand, no sculptures of comparable quality in Italy have remained exposed to the weather for seven hundred years and no sculptor could have foreseen what would happen to the surface of marble exposed over so long a period. Practical problems of expensive transport and working time would have been involved, and compromise in the choice of marble to be used may have been unavoidable in terms of the labour and finance needed. The very few marbles of the fifteenth century which can be compared with those of Giovanni in terms of sculptural achievement[12] have suffered less from exposure, but where they have long been exposed, as in the case of Donatello's statues for the Florence Cathedral Campanile, they would appear to have been cut with more perfectly tempered chisels and from more enduring stone.

The claw tool which Henry Moore has described Michelangelo as using 'like a paint brush' was either unavailable in Giovanni's day or was scarcely used. The hollowing of the backs of the Siena façade figures, and even more plainly that of the Madonna carved for the tympanum of the door of the Pisa Baptistry, shows ample evidence of drill and punch used to break up the mass of stone and facilitate its removal and no evidence of the claw tool which Michelangelo would have employed for this purpose. Once the Hellenistic technique of cutting obliquely into the block had again become fully familiar, the marble itself would suffer less stunning and would achieve, unbruised, some of the smooth luminosity to be seen in the Hermes at Olympia. This clear, unshattered skin of stone cannot be attained except by the use of a very sharp cutting edge. It was a surface greatly admired in Hellenistic, Roman and Renaissance times and inevitably led to a decline in the polychrome ornament of marble sculpture, first in the 2nd century BC and once again in the fifteenth century AD. So far as can be judged, both Nicola and his son used polychrome, with skill and discretion.[13] Giovanni's Sienese follower Tino di Camaino used it elegantly, as did his followers, but a century after them it would virtually die out as an ornament to monumental marble carvings, although it continued to be used to decorate carvings in wood.[14]

Nicola's pulpit for the Pisa Baptistry owes as much to Roman relief sculpture, whatever his debt to France, as it does to any contemporary style. For this reason he has been referred to as 'a proto-Renaissance archeologist', digging in the remote past for models. He did not need to dig, nor had he far to look, and we shall find today, gathered together in the Pisan Campo Santo, at least two of the Roman artefacts of which he made direct use, from among the many which in his day must have been decoratively scattered through the city as ostentatious evidence of Pisa's pride.

Two immediate and famous antique sources upon which he drew remain to hand within two *Fig. m* hundred yards of his pulpit. One is the low-relief, stone 'Dionysus Vase', from which he took the figure of the god supported by a satyr, adapting and modifying it from very shallow to very deep *Fig. n* relief to play the role of Simeon at the Presentation in the Temple. The other Roman treasure he *Fig. j* used is the so-called 'Hippolytus Sarcophagus' brought to Pisa in the previous century and consecrated as the tomb of the Countess Beatrice. From the left-hand portion of the main panel of this sarcophagus Nicola took the figure of Phaedra, surrounded by her attendants and by *amoretti*, as she sits at the door to the palace of Theseus at Troezen. He reversed her image, supplanted the cupid who seeks to clamber on to her knee with the Christ Child enthroned there, and replaced her attendants with the figures of Joseph and an angel. He complicated the lintel of the door and stiffened Phaedra's pose, redesigning the lines of her drapery to give her a hieratic grandeur. Thus Phaedra, no longer lustfully contemplating the nudity of Hippolytus, becomes, by *interpretatio Christiana*, the *Fig. h* Madonna receiving the Magi. In contrast to the linear convention of Italian Romanesque, the Madonna bulks out her ample robes. She occupies by implication a deep if imaginary space, nor does she do so to prove some academic point in the use of antique models; she presides in majesty as part of a divine drama.

In each of the five panels of the pulpit the narrative is set forth with Roman *gravitas* so that *Fig. k* even the dreadful solemnity of the Crucifixion imparts more of inevitability than of agony. One iconographic element in the Crucifixion, found in French ivories of a slightly earlier date but introduced here into Italian art for the first time, and never thereafter abandoned, is the joining of Christ's feet upon the cross and their attachment to the upright by a single nail. Six angle statuettes in such high relief as to be almost in the round occupy the space below the foliated quasi-Corinthian triple columns which frame the relief panels themselves. These carvings represent the Virtues and they demonstrate the ease with which classical motifs could pass into Christian iconography without offence to *Fig. l* Christian precept. The figure of Fortitude is shown as a nude Hercules wearing the skin of a slain lioness but bearing on his shoulder her living cub as a symbol of forbearance. He derives, however, at least in part, from the Hippolytus on the same sarcophagus. As the Phaedra is reversed to play her Christian role in the Adoration, so the pose of Hippolytus is partially reversed to act as Fortitude, albeit with Herculean attributes. The stance, legs, hips and torso are reversed, the arms are not. The head is proportionally enlarged, as is that of the Madonna, which may suggest a knowledge on Nicola's part of Republican no less than Imperial Roman sculpture.

How much source material was available to Nicola can only be guessed. Clearly he was capable of taking maximum advantage of whatever came to hand and if, as has been suggested, he had seen Etruscan terracotta and stone tomb figures, as he may have, he would surely have made use of them. Art history to the practising artist often proves to be treasure trove. Nicola's achievement at Pisa in fusing existing styles to create his own is a sign of that receptivity and ability uniquely to transform, for new purposes, visual information received. This might well serve as a definition of greatness in the visual arts. Exactly how he did so must remain speculative. Our knowledge of the sculptor's working drawings at this period is scanty, and it may be either that the type of schematic, linear images preserved to us in the notebook of Villard de Honnecourt served adequately to convey the necessary information from the Phaedra sarcophagus to the virgin marble block upon which Nicola's relief of the Magi was to be set out. It is also possible that clay sketch models were made. Alternatively, a drawing convention utilizing a more plastic illusion of modelling may already have been evolved for such practical problems. We do not know. Nor do we know how sophisticated were pointing methods, nor whether the taking of casts from antiques was either practised or permitted at that time. There can, however, be little doubt of the sophistication of a sculptor who could seize upon and sum up a pattern of drapery rarely to be found at that date except at Reims and Amiens and use it when he could well have been content with the drapery already existing in the Roman original.

No one was ever better entitled to inscribe below the finished work the words: *Laudetur Digne tam Bene Docta Manus* (May so learned a hand be praised as it deserves). Nicola must indeed have been learned. He had much to pass on to his son and this his son took firm hold upon, however much he later veered from parental precept. It is after the completion of the Pisa Baptistry pulpit that we are first able to detect the son at work with his father when, five years later, Nicola negotiated with Fra Melano, *Operaio* of the Cathedral of Siena, to carry out a further pulpit.

h. NICOLA PISANO. Nativity. Baptistry Pulpit, Pisa

j. Detail from the 'Hippolytus Sarcophagus'. Late Roman. Campo Santo, Pisa

k. NICOLA PISANO. Baptistry Pulpit, Pisa

l. NICOLA PISANO. *Hercules* (or *Fortitude*). Angle figure. Baptistry Pulpit. Pisa

m. Detail from 'Dionysus Vase'. Roman Augustan Period. Campo Santo, Pisa

n. NICOLA PISANO. Simeon. Detail from the Baptistry Pulpit, Pisa

o. Lion and horse. Detail from a late Roman sarcophagus. Campo Santo, Pisa

h

j

k

l

m

n

o

p

q

r

s

t

u

v

w

x

3 Giovanni, son of Nicola: Siena and Perugia

THE CONTRACT of the 29th of September 1265 between Nicola and Fra Melano stipulates the form and materials of the sumptuous new pulpit required for Siena Cathedral. It was to be ornamented with seven panels of relief carving instead of five as at Pisa. It was to be made from Carrara marble to the most detailed specification,[1] and for this labour Nicola, *magister lapidorum*, would receive eight Pisan *soldi* per day, his two pupils Arnolfo di Cambio and Lapo would each receive six *soldi* per day and – should he work – then *Iohannes filius ipsius magistri Nicoli* was to receive four *soldi* per day, to be paid to his father.

He did work and thus, in the year of the birth of Dante Alighieri, Giovanni is first contracted to engage upon the craft of marble carving. In exactly what capacity he worked we do not know. It has been suggested that since he was young and since his money was to be paid to his father, he may have played a very menial role in the workshop. We do not, however, know how young he was. Some authorities, among them Karl Frey and Adolpho Venturi,[2] date his birth as 1245; Milanesi and Pope-Hennessy give it as 'about' 1250. Bacci believes that the date 1248 can be given with some precision.[3]

In any event, fifteen – to take him at the youngest – or twenty, if he were born in 1245, was not young to be given serious responsibility in an age when the probable life-expectancy of any individual was some thirty-five years. Furthermore, it is likely that Giovanni had already spent most of his childhood in the workshop and the marble yard. Anyhow it seems he earned his four *soldi* even if it is virtually impossible to be sure how he did so or of the exact division of hands in the carving of the Siena pulpit marbles.

The whole problem of who did what upon an enterprise as complicated as the Siena pulpit tends to become a fascinating if combative game for scholars. It may be possible to judge from the style that the figures of the Liberal Arts grouped round the central column base, the Virtues on the archivolt (these in collaboration with Nicola), and the lion and lioness supports of three other columns are the work of Lapo, but such a judgement would, I suspect, in some degree stem from the fact that they are both different from and markedly inferior to any other part of the work. On existing evidence, Lapo was not a sculptor comparable in stature either to Nicola or to Arnolfo. This he proved on the Arca of S. Dominic at Bologna, if Gnudi's[4] division of that labour is to be accepted.

A detailed stylistic comparison of all the parts of the pulpit has given rise to different opinions, but anyone who has worked as part of a team upon sculpture or any large enterprise in the visual arts knows that everyone is likely to get involved with any part of the job at the direction of the guiding intelligence who master-minds it. What is more important in the case of the Siena pulpit is the ambitious extension of the iconographic programme. The Liberal Arts, whether or not they are less well carved than other parts of the pulpit, appear beneath this column for the first time in the history of Italian sculpture.[5] The development of the narrative has taken on a new urgency and the drama is played out by a far larger cast in which the majority of individuals are portrayed on a smaller scale than at Pisa. This stone *summa* is augmented by a ferocious Massacre of Innocents which was absent from the scheme at Pisa. Two of the Magi pay their visit attended by a troop of cavalry, whilst the *Fig. p* Ethiopian followers of Balthazar may be seen mounted on camels. The emotional impact of the Crucifixion is greatly intensified. At Pisa Christ crucified holds a hieratic pose hardly suspended and with *Fig. k* His arms raised as if they bore no weight. Now He hangs from the cross, His full weight taken by *Fig. r* His strained sinews, in a state of stress which prefigures Giovanni's wooden crucifixes of twenty years later, while St John gazes down intently at the joined, nailed feet and those who grieve droop with a new weight of pain. In this panel those who were responsible for the murder cower away from the cross in a new realization of what has been done. The Last Judgement on the Siena pulpit occupies two complete panels of relief, with Christ the Judge as the angle figure. He is in the act of speaking *Fig. q* and here too, despite His gentle countenance, the particular intensity of His delivery of judgement prefigures the intensity of 'visible speech' which Giovanni would later impart to the colloquium of marble Prophets and Sibyls on the façade of Siena Cathedral.

It is a measure of the intellectual and emotional change of attitude which seems to have taken place in these years towards the nature of the impact which narrative sculpture was intended to convey, that a new emphasis is laid both upon the position of Christ on the cross and upon the urgency mixed with compassion of His spoken judgement. That His Word should inspire such a dreadful and palpable apprehension among those who crucified Him and those who wait upon His judgement differs in kind from the foregone conclusion as to who could and who could not be sure of salvation, which earlier obtained. Conceivably it was this all too real uncertainty which would carry Giovanni to greatness and it is prophetically to be encountered in his father's work when father and son first worked together upon the Pulpit of Siena Cathedral.

The sculptor's impulse is to create forms which convince him, and convince those who contemplate his work, of the 'reality' of his vision – the true source of his inspiration – whether physically or mystically experienced. From his power to be convinced will depend the conviction his work will carry to others. If the life beyond death is more important to the sculptor and the society to which he belongs than the material world, then his inevitable reference to the material world in order to create visible imagery will not be a sum of physical particulars, even though a work of sculpture must have a physical existence. Since it is his function to make images, he will make pre-eminently symbolic images, striving to convey the essence, if necessary at the expense of the facts. To the early medieval mind, saturated with symbolism and convinced of the illusory nature of material things, the spiritual world was real, as the physical world was not. Not only faith but reason sustained this proposition. Of no great 'truth' was the medieval mind more conscious than that of St Paul when he said that now we see through a glass darkly but then face to face. The Middle Ages never forgot that all things would be absurd if their meaning were exhausted in their function and that their place in the phenomenal world, if by their essence they did not reach into a world beyond this, would be without meaning. Thus Huizinga[6] makes the point that the material world was something seen by medieval man through a glass darkly. What lay beyond would be seen face to face. But the evolution of nominalism, casting, as it did, doubts on this unity of faith and reason, produced a concentration upon 'the reality of particulars' which tended to erode belief in the generalizations which could adequately be conveyed by a wholly symbolic art.

The concentration of the artist upon physical particulars, the material details of the world about him, which developed in the thirteenth century had the gradual but enormously consequential effect of removing the dark glass and supplanting it at least with the illusion, if not with the fact, that he experienced the world face to face. The consequence was not only to allow him to 'see' the natural world as meaningful but to find himself at the centre of it and thus to find the human body and the human face meaningful in its particulars not only in configuration but in the psychological states of the individual conveyed by the disposition of these particulars in the individual countenance. If these states could not be rationalized they were real enough to be convincingly portrayed, being more real than rational concepts.

The reassertion of the validity and importance of physical appearances did not occur overnight. It began in the thirteenth century and has continued, but a crucial phase in its development occurred in the work of Nicola and Giovanni. If the learned programme of Nicola's first pulpit was made more visually convincing by references back to Roman funerary reliefs as the readiest available means to portray the 'reality' of appearances, that reality was vested in types rather than in individuals. The persons portrayed are generalizations. In his Siena Pulpit a more personal and emotional response to individuals is in evidence, and portraiture, that specific concentration on the particularity of the individual, is foreshadowed. The revival of portraiture would follow a lapse of more than a millennium and it was the product first of High Scholasticism[7] and thereafter of Critical Nominalism which grew out of that Scholasticism. These philosophical concepts would lead not only to the revival of the portrait, but before that to the creation of images with which the human individual could so identify himself that he could find in the contemplation of them new means of relating himself to God. In the creation of works of sculpture for such homage by empathy, Giovanni remains unsurpassed.

At the opposite pole to scholasticism and yet essentially as an aspect of the same concern with pre-eminent values, stood a movement dedicated to severing any tie between reason and faith, with a view to discarding reason as incompatible with the integrity of faith. At its most irrational this tendency proved hysterically influential at exactly the time with which we are here concerned, for it was in 1260 that the chiliastic prophecies which had developed from the writings of Joachim da Fiore[8] were to be realized and the reign of the Church would come to an end, to be replaced by the Age of the Everlasting Gospel. These prophecies were not, of course, realized, yet their influence continued to be felt until late in the sixteenth century. Fostered by the Spirituals, the activist wing of the Franciscan Order, Joachim's doctrines were held tenaciously by those who clung to the first principles of St Francis and many apocryphal writings were fathered upon him.

Awareness of impending apocalypse is a climate familiar to twentieth-century man. The effects of apprehension, of the imminent collapse of an existing order, make their mark upon whole generations, and Giovanni Pisano belonged to such a generation. In his time the very rock upon which the Church stood seemed threatened, a situation as menacing to medieval man as our own apocalyptic threat has seemed to us. To any generation the past is secure, and in his comparatively recent past medieval man had conceived reality in terms almost exactly opposed to our own. To him the physical world had been a temporary way station if not a passing dream, whilst the world of the spirit was to him the reality. Such a sense of the impermanence and even inconsequence of the material world can readily be borne if eternity rests assured, but in questioning the existence of universals the Critical Nominalists created an alarm which mysticism alone could assuage, and a mystical intoxication with divinity can be a serious threat to established order. Doubt and discord led to conflict between the monastic orders. Messianic fanaticism led to wild disorders which were followed by suppression. Activists such as the Spirituals and even more extreme cults such as the Flagellants who after 1260 ranged across Europe in bands calling for penitence under the lash, were active long before the Black Death of 1348 seemed to confirm the wrath of God. It was this cataclysm which truly brought the Middle Ages to an end but to the climate of ideas which might seem to predicate such an apocalypse, Giovanni, no less than other thinking men, was subject. Nevertheless Giovanni's art had strong classical elements which ordered his emotional responses to the art of sculpture.

The word 'classical' has come to possess a confusing variety of meanings. In its most general usage, it is applied to works of art or literature (but not to music where the term means something else again) which survive from antiquity or which derive from antique models, as does Nicola's pulpit. In another sense it is used to convey the quality, which Berenson described as 'existential' or 'the ineloquent in art',[9] of a concentration on the part of the artist upon ordered formal qualities austerely purged of rhetoric. The latter use of the term stands counter to the term 'romantic', where emotional intensity of expression has become the artist's primary aim. Confusion arises where a work from the Greek or Roman world is eloquent and rhetorical, since it is then 'classical' in the first sense but 'romantic' in the second, as are the Laocoön or the Pergamon Altar. Nicola's Pisa Baptistry pulpit is classical in both senses of the word: his Siena pulpit is less so in both senses and certain of his son's sculpture conveys emotional intensity of enormous power but seldom if ever loses its classical discipline.

It is customary to contrast the classicism of Nicola with his son's vigorous rejection of it in favour of a passionately expressive 'Gothic' style. I believe this to be an over-simplification. It seems to me that Nicola himself moved, within his mature style, towards a classicism which was less Apollonian and more Dionysiac, and that French influence was persuasive in promoting this shift of style. Lacking specific evidence to the contrary, it might be assumed that Nicola was aware of the conflict between the Thomist and Augustinian trends which I have briefly described. It may even have disturbed him. Assuming too that Nicola was in agreement with, if not in full control of, both the sculpture and the programme of the Siena pulpit, then Giovanni, in his most formative years, was brought face to face not only with a theological and scholastic dichotomy but with the problem inherent in these conflicting doctrines as to the validity of natural appearances as vehicles for emotional and religious expression. Overtly, all that there is to go on at this stage of Giovanni's career is his father's modification of style between the Pisa and Siena pulpits. If, however, the change were more profound, then the son's development is less obviously a rift with the father's attitude of mind than has often been supposed.

The seeds of Giovanni's *terribilità*, together with his capacity to convey heartbreaking tenderness in his Madonna groups, are foreseeable in his father's Siena pulpit. Perhaps as Giovanni grew older the threat of the apocalypse clashed more and more fiercely against the citadel of reason, the Apollonian fell back before the assault of the Dionysiac, the need to create images of empathy became more intense and the superficial means at hand to make the transition apparent were French and Gothic. We cannot know the extent to which either father or son felt the conflict, nor how fiercely each debated in his mind the spiritual crisis of the times in which they lived. On the basis of the evidence of the sculpture he made, perhaps it would not be impossibly rash to suggest that what may have been to Nicola a mere cause for concern came to afflict Giovanni with increasing severity as he grew older.

Nor did the shadow of the apocalypse hang over Giovanni's world in a spiritual sense alone. The age through which he lived would increasingly seem to darken under the wrath of God and daily life was threatened by momentous change. A population increase of inexplicable magnitude would occur in Tuscany, to be redressed by a sequence of famines and plagues, and if those calamities still lay in the future as the young Giovanni worked with his father in Siena Cathedral, I do not find it easy to believe that, in an age of portents, he was insensible to them. A great sculptor's style is not formed solely by aesthetics. It is also the product of a special awareness in which fore-knowledge can play a part.

Work on the Siena pulpit was concluded by 1268, when Nicola signed a final quittance on be-half of himself and his son. Arnolfo di Cambio appears then to have left Nicola's workshop and in due course set up his own workshop in Rome. Nicola himself, having completed not only the pulpit, but coincidentally the Arca of St Dominic for San Domenico Maggiore at Bologna, in which the bones of the Saint were placed in 1267, is believed to have returned with his son to Pisa, but between 1268 and 1277, when father and son were again at work together, nothing is known of Giovanni. It was during that time that he may have travelled to Paris and visited other parts of France. There is no documentary evidence that he did.[10] If, however, he had arrived in Paris in *c.* 1270, it would have been at the beginning of the end of the phase called High Scholasticism which is generally marked for convenience's sake by historians as coinciding with the death of Saint Louis. He would presumably have gravitated towards the school of Notre Dame, the centre of intellectual and artistic life of the city, where he would have encountered arguments fiercely engaged as to the validity of the revival of Augustinianism with its assertion of the independence of the will from the intellect, as opposed to the synthetic power of reason upon which Aquinas had founded his arguments. That Giovanni was a sculptor and neither a professional theologian nor an academic philosopher may deter aesthetes from believing that he, a medieval master-mason, would bother with these involved speculations. I do not insist that he did, even supposing he was ever in Paris, but if he was he would probably have attended those disputations which were, to men of intelligence in late medieval times, both as enter-tainment and as stimulus much what the theatre and 'highbrow' television are to us. He would have attended these disputations because he was obviously not a fool, because they were instruc-tive and exciting and perhaps, most important of all, because there was a very close and very positive connection between the problems and dilemmas of theology, philosophy and the arts of architecture and sculpture.

When, in 1269, Aquinas returned to Paris from Naples, the rift between philosophy and theol-ogy had become a chasm. And by implication this rift was of great significance to the form that sculpture should take. As Gordon Leff puts it,[11] 'the study of Aristotle had broken through the safe-guards to faith which Aquinas had erected' and the philosophers who were drawn to Averroes' pagan interpretation of Aristotle were vociferous in dislocating the two disciplines from one another.

Aquinas and Bonaventura joined in condemning this heterodox division between philosophy and theology, seeking to dispel what they believed to be dangerous errors resulting from a mistaken refusal to recognize the differences between levels of truth. Such differences, they maintained, must not be suppressed, else those who pursued them must inevitably affirm that reason was *contrary* to faith.

The full crisis came in 1277 when Aquinas was condemned *post mortem* for contradicting St Augustine, largely because he had argued that the philosopher had embarked on a procedure in thought that was not simply a disagreement in the matter of ideas but another and dangerously separate standard of truth which could not be integrated with faith. 'The year 1277', as Leff goes on, 'was a catalyst. Like all upheavals it cleared neither the air nor men's minds. Instead of a new era of a now clearly defined body of admissible theological and philosophical doctrines there was flux.'

Into this flux, in the seventies, a young and intelligent sculptor in Paris, where the argument waxed hottest, would have been plunged. The question with which he would have been faced would have been that of the legitimacy of the form in which the visual information (which sculpture was designed to convey) should be conveyed, for upon the intellectual control of the will depends the clear sculptural description of natural forms, whereas upon the intensity of the faith and its emotional power to inspire, must depend the impact that sculpture must have upon the faithful. It is neither a trivial nor an irrelevant question in the context. The growing necessity for empathy in the spectator's relationship to the marble was also a new factor.

Added to this, Giovanni would have been concerned with style. He would have arrived at a time when, from Paris and other centres of intellectual and creative vitality, the influence of the French style was moving vigorously not only eastwards towards Germany, northwards to England, but towards Italy in the south. A trickle of French ivory carvings had begun to flow south which, by the turn of the century, would have become a substantial stream.

If Giovanni went to France and saw at first hand, in Paris or Amiens or Reims or Sens, the monumental cathedral sculpture which appears to have played an important part in forming his own mature style, he did so at a significant moment in the history of ideas and at a time, in his early twenties, when he would have been highly receptive to them.

By 1276 he was certainly back in Italy and his first wholly independent sculpture dates from this period.[12] In its innovations it is independent to a remarkable degree. Originally a half-length figure of *Pl. 118*   the Madonna holding the Child on her hip, she was extended to three-quarter length by the addition of a separate section to increase her monumentality. Far more important, with a subtle twist of the figure of the Mother towards the Child, Giovanni created a wholly individual and, in Italy, an unprecedented image of the human relationship between them. They confront one another with marvellous tenderness, looking into one another's eyes. The curving veil which circles from below the Virgin's crown to lead our eyes across to the Child may be a device taken from the Tomb of Constance d'Arles in St Denis, the carving of her face and brow may owe something to the sculptors of Reims, the mouth may recall Nicola's hand, but the conception is Giovanni's. The empathy, by which they may be worshipped, is Giovanni's creation and is centred in the glance exchanged between Mother and Child. It is centred in the eyes and eyelids so much more closely observed and less schematic in treatment than any French counterpart. These would have been the features to make the most immediate impact upon those who first looked up at Mary and her Son in the tympanum over the door for which she was designed. Much is lost to us when we view her in her present position, set at the wrong height upon a clumsy modern plinth in the Pisan Campo Santo, but even this cannot destroy the miracle of that gentle confrontation. This carving was the first of a series of Madonnas which occur throughout Giovanni's career like moments of supernatural rest during his long contest with his art.

During 1277, Giovanni was at work on the great Fountain of Perugia which still stands in the main square of that city. In this work he played a role which, if it were not equal to his father's in conception, may well have been greater in actual execution.

Times had changed. The Ghibelline cause, already undermined by the death of the Emperor Frederick, had been irreparably damaged when Manfred, his heir, was killed at Benevento in 1266 and it was subsequently shattered when the army of the Empire was routed at Tagliacozzo in 1268. Siena was bloodily converted to the Guelph party and Perugia, a Guelph stronghold, entered a period of civic affluence which, among other things, prompted the foundation of her university.

Among the outward manifestations of Perugia's rise were the commissioning of the Fontana Maggiore and a new aqueduct to bring water to it. Nicola and his son, despite their Pisan citizenship and the Ghibelline affiliations of Pisa, were awarded the contract and undertook this substantial labour. Whether or not they, as Pisans, were personally concerned with the political situation we cannot know. It is customary to regard artists as indifferent to such matters. Nevertheless, the destruction of the Empire as a major rival to the Church, and the consequent rise of the independent city commune, is reflected in the sculpture of the Perugia Fountain by the inclusion of representations of Ernano di Sasseferrato, the *capitano del popolo*, and Matteo da Correggio, *podestà della città*, among the upright high-reliefs at the angles of the upper basin. Such 'portraits' of dignitaries do not occur in north Italian art prior to this date, although they are to some extent prefigured in the Imperial sculpture of Frederick II's Capuan Gate, where the personification of cities as human figures also occurs.

The Fontana Maggiore may be directly interpreted by reference to the *Speculum majus* of Vincent of Beauvais, *c.* 1250. Vincent stipulated that fallen humanity begins the work of redemption by manual labour, especially the tilling and harvesting of the soil at every season of the year. Once again this choice of motif for a fountain reflects the direct connection between the baptismal font and the utilitarian fountain. The 'Months' occur on fonts, sometimes combined with the signs of the Zodiac as at St Evroult de Montfort (Orne), *c.* 1200. Antelami's 'Months' were carved as exterior

Continued on page 53

2

3

4

5

6

7

8

9

10

11

12

13

14

15

16

17

18

19

20

21

22

23

24

25

26   27   28   29   30   31

32   33   34   35   36   37

38

39

40

41

42

43

44

45

46

47

48

49

50

51

52

53

54

55

56

57

58

59

60

61

62

63

Full notes to the plates are on page 207

decorations for the Parma Baptistry itself, a further example of the close and natural symbolic conjunction of fountain and baptistry.

'On the Fontana Maggiore... the Months and Sciences in combination with scenes from Genesis make up a history of the world. But local traditions also play a part in this history. In one of the bas-reliefs, Romulus and Remus are a reminder of the fabulous beginning of Rome, mother of civilisation. The statuettes of the upper basin recall the origins of Augusta Perusia herself ... the (Trojan) hero Aulestes, legendary king of Etruria, progenitor of the race, stands near the saints Herculanus and Lawrence who later awakened it to Christian life.'[13] As such the Fountain intermingles all four of the great medieval scholarly traditions, the historical, the physical, the moral and the encyclopedic, and in this latter particular – the medieval obsession with *scientia universalis* – the programme of the Perugia Fountain, like the Pisani pulpits, contains a *summa*.

The fountain, long in preparation as a hydraulic problem, was apparently executed with remarkable rapidity as an architectural and sculptural one. Like Nicola's pulpits, it is polygonal in form and as such derives from the concept of the fountains in Paradise. It consists of two superimposed stone basins surmounted by a round one in bronze from which rises a bronze group of caryatids in turn supporting two bronze lions and two gryphons. These may once have carried a further small bronze basin. The lower basin, a twenty-five-sided polygon, bears fifty low reliefs, for the face of each side is divided into two. These reliefs, which owe much to the antique and something to the Romanesque-Byzantine 'Months' beside the entrance to the Pisa Baptistry, display three closed cycles, one, of twenty-four panels, representing the Months and Signs of the Zodiac, another the eight Liberal Arts and the third, a group of fifteen biblical, historical and mythological scenes including two illustrating Aesop's fables. Each panel bears a titular inscription and each cycle is closed with reliefs either of lions, gryphons or eagles, one of the latter being superscribed with the words *Boni Joannis et (?) Scultoris Huius Operis*.

The upper basin displays upright high reliefs of individual figures representing saints, sinners, prophets and personifications of the Church, Victory, Theology, Lake Trasimeno, Perugia and Chiusi, and portraits of the two civic dignitaries already mentioned. Between these twenty-four reliefs, which resemble the angle sculptures of the Siena pulpit, the faces of the twelve sides of the polygon are left blank. From the centre, a stone column rises bearing the bronze basin containing the one bronze group which can be connected directly with Nicola and Giovanni Pisano. It was cast by the lost-wax process and is signed by one 'Rubeus', presumably the bronze founder.

As the sole surviving work in metal to have been designed by either Giovanni or his father, it has been greatly admired and some authorities attribute it to the hand of one or other of these masters. There is, however, no proof that either actually modelled the wax and although the conception is noble and the heads and hands are finely wrought, the group is hardly comparable in formal mastery to the stone carving of either Nicola or Giovanni. If the latter's reputation as a goldsmith were well founded, it seems unlikely that he would have been so inadequate a modeller and I suspect that unless he worked upon the waxes of the heads and hands, he had no part in the actual manufacture of the bronze, which may be the unaided work of 'Rubeus' or based on designs by Giovanni, which in turn are based upon the antique. If on the other hand the bronze was designed by Nicola (and it relates in form to a holy water basin at Pistoia designed by Nicola but executed by Lapo in 1270), the proportions of the figures do not seem typical of his work.

The bronze lion and gryphon symbols of Perugia which, before the restoration of the Fountain in 1949, surmounted the caryatids, show a muscularity and a surface tension lacking in the caryatids. *Pls. 12, 13* The group is comparable to the carving of a gryphon, an eagle and a lion at the base of the central column of the Pistoia pulpit and, like the eight surviving bronze animal-head protomes which jut from *Pl. 153* the upper stone basin, argue their execution under Giovanni's eye, if they are not from his hand.[14] *Pls. 4–11*

The speed with which the whole enterprise was carried out suggests a large workshop and many hands working under an energetic and demanding master. There has been much conjecture as to the division of the work, and the rhymed inscription which records the date of the completion of the fountain bears the names of one Fra Bevegnato, and Bonisegna the hydraulics engineer, together with that of Nicola 'the finest flower of honest sculptors' and Giovanni his 'most dear son'. Considering Nicola's probable age and the far from clement climate of Perugia, it is reasonable to suppose that Giovanni in the prime of life took upon himself the practical burdens of execution and the discipline of the workshop, whilst Nicola was responsible for the design and architecture of the whole. Since no other work from Nicola's final phase of activity has been securely identified, no comparison of style can be made, and although it is pure conjecture, perhaps derived from my reading as it were between the lines of the inscription, there seems to me a special and grateful affection implied by the phrase: *Genitus carissimus imus cui si non dampnes nomen dic esse Iohannes* of an old man who records how he has placed his trust in his beloved son.

The Fontana Maggiore was apparently damaged by earthquake either in 1340 or 1438, or both. It was incorrectly restored in 1471 and reconstructed in 1948–9. Apart from the weathering of certain of the low reliefs and the replacement with copies of the corner relief figure of Melchisedek, it appears, after six hundred and ninety years, as impressive and functional as it was when it was finished in 1278, although it gives the appearance today of having been overcleaned with abrasives.

After the completion of the fountain no more is heard of Nicola in life. A document witnessed by Giovanni, *quondam magistri Nicholi*, proves that he was no longer living in 1284.

Vasari relates that 'becoming old, Nicola retired to Pisa, leaving the management of all their labours to his son' and had done so before the fountain was executed. He also tells us of a tomb for Pope Urban IV 'who had expired about that time in Perugia', for which Giovanni was responsible but which had been destroyed when the Cathedral was enlarged,[15] and he goes on to relate that after completing the fountain Giovanni's journey home was delayed by a visit to Florence, where he assisted in the construction of some mills on the Arno. It was in Florence that he learned of his father's death and returning at last to Pisa, 'he was received with great honour by all the city, everyone rejoicing that, although Nicola had passed away, yet Giovanni remained to them, the heir to his virtues as well as to his abilities.'[16] Nor were the Pisans disappointed in their expectations.

4 *The First Sculptures for the Pisa Baptistry*

WITHOUT the external sculpture for the Pisa Baptistry with which Giovanni was occupied after his return from Perugia and again on his return from Siena in 1297, I should not have received the shock of awe which I have described and which first prompted Henry Moore to feel the need to publish our homage to him. This chapter therefore is the core of the book because, despite the quality of the pulpits at Pistoia and in the Cathedral at Pisa, despite the splendour of the Madonna groups and the majesty still remaining to the fragments of the tomb of Margaret of Luxembourg at Genoa, Giovanni's monumental sculptures are to me his highest achievement, even if what remains to us are the ghosts of it.

The finest and best preserved of the monumental half-length figures from the first tier of the Pisa Baptistry are now ranged round the inner wall of that building one metre from the ground. They are colossal statues in terms of their period, being between 165 and 184 cm. in height, and they give an impression of being incomparably more vast than they actually are. They differ not only in scale from those of the Siena façade but in design, for they were carved to occupy deep niches. They conduct no dialogue and do not mirror one another's actions.

Pls. 64–6, 71–79

Unlike the full-length Siena sculptures, discussed in Chapter 6, these Baptistry colossi are in very high relief and not carved wholly in the round.[1] They are without the extraordinary torsions and dramatic action of the Siena façade sculptures and have, until recently, received far less attention, yet they are unique in their time as essays in the penetration of the psychology of the individual in sculpture, despite their scale and their present condition. The limitations imposed by the niche and by the formal generalization required to make the figures 'read' so far above eye level, might well have

Notes on p. 203

prompted conventional, generalized images. Nothing is further from the case. These great marbles describe the character of each prophet and evangelist with the uncanny analysis of individual personality to be found in Rembrandt's late 'portraits' of saints.

Once again, and for the last time, the division of labour between Giovanni and his father remains in question. Nicola is known to have worked on external sculpture for the Baptistry in 1265 and some authorities[2] tentatively ascribe many of the colossi to Nicola. Pope-Hennessy suggests that the Madonna and Child which occupied the niche above the door may have been Nicola's last and largest work. It is my belief that this, the four evangelists and the four prophets, now to be seen within the Baptistry, breathe the spirit of Giovanni, whatever part Nicola played in their initial conception. We do not know exactly what Nicola contributed to the façade in and after 1265 and we have no other sculpture on such a scale from his hand with which to compare these colossal figures. It is possible that Nicola worked on the colossi while Giovanni was abroad, as he may have been, in the period between 1268 and 1279. On the other hand, nothing we know by Nicola suggests that particular concern with the temperament, the personality of each individual which is portrayed in these images. What remain to us are the nine great half-length figures now in the Baptistry itself and the twenty-one full-length figures, on average 121 cm. in height, removed from the pinnacles above the main tier of niches in 1846 and placed in the Museo San Matteo at Pisa, together with three busts, between 77 and 92 cm. in height, from the pinnacles over the east portal.

The full-length figures were undoubtedly executed after Giovanni's return from Siena and therefore some years after Nicola's death, but they are by no means all of equal quality. The finest of them, however, have that vitality and dynamic invention which Giovanni alone could release from the stone. These are the sculptures which initially moved Henry Moore to recognize Giovanni's greatness, just as the colossal figures from the same site moved me. It is ironical that both he and I were startled into this recognition by seeing the sculptures at eye level: possibly neither of us would have become aware of them had they remained in place upon the Baptistry. It is not, I think, remarkable that independently both Moore and I recognized that Giovanni Pisano should stand beside Michelangelo in the personal pantheon every sculptor builds in his own mind.

Giovanni and Michelangelo have more in common than their greatness, even if any comparison between them must take into account that they belonged to different centuries, thought differently about theological no less than sculptural problems and enjoyed different degrees of fame. Despite this, they irresistibly invite comparison with one another, not only in temperament and in *terribilità*, but in the frustration which dogged them both. Michelangelo made his complaints known both in his letters and sonnets and to his biographers. Giovanni, save for one inscription on his final pulpit, remains silent. After Michelangelo's Promethean crisis, his tragic inability to complete came to be equated with the supreme liberty an artist could possess: the liberty to fail. This liberty, even if after Michelangelo the combination of vanity and humility which can prompt a man to view a perfectly completed work as *hubris* – a vain rivalry with God – became something of an aesthetic convention, was certainly not a conceit acceptable in Giovanni's day. Yet he too might be said to have earned that supreme liberty. To support this supposition, I shall call the 'Moses' of Michelangelo to witness and metaphorically try to set it beside that of Giovanni, not in terms of comparison of style, which would be idle, but in terms of how each master interpreted the implications and summed up in sculpture the nature of that archetypal prophet.

Freud, in the most truly perceptive essay he wrote about a work of art,[3] pointed out that in Michelangelo's Moses both doubt and a sense of inadequacy are expressed by the precarious position of the tablets held unstably beneath Moses' right arm and the prophet's oddly uneasy grip upon his beard. Not being an art-historian, Freud felt at liberty to analyse the sculpture on the assumption that Michelangelo understood the psychological condition of Moses at a crucial moment in his life. Freud, indeed, wrote as if this comprehension of the nature of an archetype, expressed at so profound a level, was the clue to the greatness of the sculpture, rather than its purely sculptural qualities.

Superficially, Michelangelo's Moses appears as a figure of Renaissance grandeur, his vast physique symbolizing a vast spiritual power to command. At first glance the sculpture seems to present some Olympian rival to Jove but further contemplation reveals the image of a man in desperation, a man in danger of allowing the commandments themselves to slip from his grasp, who feels his own hopes slip from him, despite his piety and the strength of his faith. He is at once heroic and fallible.

Giovanni Pisano's Moses, carved two centuries earlier, is in no such doubt. He is the epitome of *Pl. 76* greatness in defeat. His head is wearily inclined, fatigue consumes him. He points to the tablets but although he still holds them firmly, he seems to supplicate his people to read and to obey as if he knew that the commandments would not be kept, as if he himself had lost the very power of command which had made him great. Failure is written on his face. Yet Moses led the children of Israel to the promised land. Giovanni knew, as Michelangelo knew, as we know, that he was not permitted to enter it. Both sculptors are here concerned with images of doubt. If Michelangelo came to doubt his own genius and said so in his sonnets, we deal here with a sculptor who, I submit, came as near to a similar confession as his times permitted.

Of all Michelangelo's powers, the highest is his power to inspire awe, an awe which springs not only from the grandeur of his art but from the implacable supernormality of the beings his vision brought forth. It is not fanciful to conceive, with an artist of such a stature, that he himself was in awe of his own vision and spent his inner life uneasily balanced between defiance and submission to the God only he could envision. I suggest that Giovanni endured a comparably lonely singularity. His Moses is no less uneasy than Michelangelo's, although he is older and more resigned to defeat. His David is also older than Michelangelo's mighty adolescent and he is an image of an individual *Pl. 75, Fig. v* grown more complex with age, but, if all aesthetic comparisons are left aside, and both sculptures are examined as studies in the psychology of an individual, then Michelangelo's David could be

Giovanni's in youth, and the condition of youth – that Renaissance preoccupation – was less interesting to Giovanni than to Michelangelo.

The Renaissance Florentines saw David as a boy in contest with Goliath; Giovanni saw him as a prophet and a king. He gives us the king by means of the Hellenistic device of exaggerating the thickness of the neck, but he also gives us the David beloved of Jonathan, the David of whom Saul was jealous and afraid. In his carving of the brow he gives us the prophet and the poet and by his carving of the mouth and chin, the treacherous and sentimental adulterer, who forgave his treacherous son and wept for him after his death.[4] And in the same image we may find David the lawgiver, who was also the zealot despised by his wife, who was the psalmist of Israel yet whose house was not as the light of the morning, whose house the Lord made not to grow. Yet Giovanni's marble portrayal of this complex and disturbed individual seems, in David's own last words, to be 'springing out of the earth by clear shining after rain'.

The David of Giovanni Pisano tells us more about David than any Renaissance image, for the great sword hand laid to mute the strings of the harp is the hand of a giant-killer who no longer needs to show his muscles, and the sculptor reveals him with incredible subtlety considering the bulk and the worn condition of the stone. For centuries this statue showed its subtlety only to God, for who could discern it, in this slab of stone, from a distance of 140 feet? To me, the singer who silences his harp evokes the intrinsic silence of sculpture itself and yet contains the 'speaking' likeness.

I have digressed at length to discuss two specific statues by Giovanni because they were the first that brought me to my knees and because I am more concerned with the nature of the person revealed in the image than I am with the purely formal aspect of it. As a twentieth-century sculptor perhaps I should not be, but I am.

I am also concerned to deduce from these images something of the nature of the sculptor since, self-evidently, the artist identifies with his subject and, whether intentionally or not, his examination and communication of it reveal him. With Giovanni we have little evidence beyond the sculpture to go on, but what we have first emerges tantalizingly and incompletely from his next major commission. The circumstances which frustrated his career as a sculptor on a monumental scale are sufficiently recorded to allow us to see him plunged into a sea of troubles. We do not, however, precisely know what they were. We know that he left Pisa between March 1284 and September 1285 and in leaving renounced his Pisan citizenship, a far from insignificant act. We do not know why. Conceivably his decision was affected by the disastrous defeat Pisa suffered in 1284 at the battle of Meloria[5] when she was overwhelmingly defeated by Genoa and thus increased the rapidity of that decline from greatness which eventually came to end in her subjection to Florence. It may simply have been a condition attaching to an attractive offer from Siena. At all events, in 1284 Giovanni took Sienese citizenship and despite some uncertainty as to whether he took up residence there before 1287, he concentrated his activity on work for the Sienese during the next ten years.

The Pisa Baptistry

*In the Baptistry and in the
Museo San Matteo*

Full notes to the plates are on page 211

80

81

85

86

87

88

89

90

5 *The Decade at Siena*

THERE ARE a fair number of extant documents concerning Giovanni's activities in Siena but they are sufficiently cryptic to have stimulated much learned argument. Furthermore, the meagre narrative which may be constructed from these documents leaves various important questions unanswered. Firstly, he was granted not only citizenship but immunities both from all taxes and from military duties, apparently before he began any work, but in the document granting these privileges Giovanni is given only the title of *magister* and not that of *caput magistrorum*. As there was precedent for the listing of qualifications and of rank in awarding citizenship, this omission is unusual. Furthermore, the extent and nature of his duties were not noted. In 1284 the Chapter's intention seems to have been to construct 'a simple façade' for the Cathedral, but in January 1285 a resolution was passed by the fifteen Governors of the City to the effect that Fra Magio, the *Operaio* or Clerk of Works of the Cathedral, together with the Mercantile Consuls and three Councillors of the Cathedral Works should consult with the Bishop about work to be undertaken on the building and that their decision should be acted

Notes on p. 204 upon. It may be assumed on this basis, in concordance with the relevant passage in Vasari,[1] plus Giovanni's citizenship and immunities, that this discussion touched on what work he should undertake. What remains obscure is that the resolution refers to work *ante maiorum ecclesiam*, which seems to concern work in front of the church as opposed to that upon the façade itself, which is elsewhere invariably referred to as *facies ecclesiae*. No other document has been found which refers to Giovanni's initial work on the Duomo. He may have made a model of the proposed façade by 1285, or he may not. We do not know.

A documentary gap follows until August 1287, when Giovanni witnessed an agreement in which Fra Magio undertook to borrow money for work on a mill. Here again Giovanni receives only the title *magister*. In September, a further document concerning payment for a *fenestra rotunda magna* for the Cathedral was drafted. This window and the orientation of the façade itself has been the subject of debate,[2] but no one can say for certain either what was originally intended by the Cathedral authorities, what the work was to be like or whether Giovanni had a free hand in designing it. The documents suggest that in leaving these vital details unspecified some of those delays, disputes and the personal animosities which can arise when large building work is undertaken by civic committees had already developed.

In no surviving Sienese document is Giovanni specifically contracted, a fact in remarkable contrast to the precision with which the form of his father's pulpit had been prescribed by the august officials of the same city at an earlier date. Instead we are next presented with documents arising from the imposition of a collaborator in the work on the façade. It may be inferred from this that Giovanni had been at work for some time as acting, if not titular, *capomaestro* and it is possible that it was the fact that he had not been established in this rank, that he was the victim of the law's delays, the insolence of office and other intolerable irritations of which we know nothing which prompted the somewhat apologetic note that this new and surely unwelcome colleague was not to interfere with the work upon which Giovanni was already engaged. The man upon whom this modest limitation of action was placed was a Sienese who had returned to his native city after a period of exile for adultery. His name was Ramo di Paganello and he was held in such local esteem that presumably he was pardoned for vices working in his flesh, by reason of his virtues in working stone. Clearly the authorities favoured him highly, for they not only hired Ramo but allowed him to hire his brothers and nephews to work upon the fabric. Ramo received a master's wage of six *soldi* per working day, whilst his assistants were paid in accordance with the going rate.

It is possible that Giovanni equably accepted Ramo and his brood, but it does not seem likely, for Giovanni at no time emerges as a modest or amenable man and presumably he was well advanced upon the general programme of sculpture for the new façade. *Capomaestro* or not, he was a master in high standing and in the murky light of events a proud and touchy one. Doubtless he had made enemies and possibly one of those factions, whose obstinate and often savage activities bedevil medieval Italian history, was aligned against him. He could be forgiven if he had felt himself intolerably insulted. As for Ramo di Paganello, he must have had outstanding talent as a sculptor and he had spent his exile in France where we may suppose he had diligently acquired those fashionable French novelties of style much in demand in Tuscany at that date, with which Giovanni had earlier made himself familiar. Rivalry is implicit in the situation, but what we do not know is why Ramo was welcomed with such enthusiasm in Siena in November 1287 on his return to his native city. Furthermore, no single work of sculpture which can positively be identified remains to show us how great a master he was. We know that he subsequently worked at Orvieto both in 1293 and, after

Fig. v

Pl. 122

a sojourn in Naples, in 1314. One work of consequence has been attributed to him by Enzo Carli,[3] a Madonna and Child in wood, now in the Cathedral Museum at Orvieto; this leads to further problems for it has been confidently suggested that this piece, which Carli dates to the first decade of the *trecento*, was the model for part of a late marble group by Giovanni, now in fragments – the 'Madonna di Arrigo', carved for the Emperor Henry VII between 1312 and 1313.[4] This latter sculpture was profoundly influential and was copied by Giovanni's best-known pupil, Tino da Camaino. If Ramo really originated this work, then Giovanni admired Ramo and if jealousy also played a part in the earlier intrigue we shall probably never know how it affected the issue. It is very difficult to judge from this small wooden Madonna, supposing it to be by Ramo, what Ramo's work as a monumental sculptor in marble was really like, and even less can we judge how able were the rest of his family. What remains visible to us of the first stages of the Siena Cathedral façade and the mighty sculpture intended for it reveals the personality of one artist of genius in complete domination of the scheme, and that is surely Giovanni Pisano rather than Ramo di Paganello.

By an odd irony, as matters go from bad to worse for Giovanni during his ill-fated career at Siena, he achieved appropriate titular recognition within six months of being condemned and harshly penalized for a crime of which we do not know the nature. Sentence was passed upon him in January 1290 by the *Podestà* Giovanni Accorimbono and on July 17th in the same year, the General Council of the Campana met to deal, among other issues, with this unfortunate affair. At once, the Council commuted the sentence and referred to Giovanni as *caput magistrorum* and as a man 'most useful and necessary to the work on the Cathedral'. He was therefore to make a 'gift' to the Madonna of 600 lire and would then be absolved of all further penalties and need not fear seizure. This 'gift', increased by a fine of 200 lire, was at once paid to the *Biccherna* of the Commune by the *Operaio* of the Cathedral, Fra Iacopo Angioleri, who two weeks later implored the Council to advance money for further work on the Cathedral. They did so, assigning the sum of 800 lire for the purpose and thus bringing the financial situation of the *caput magistrorum* back to square one.

During the next seven years, apart from a brief visit to Pisa in the summer of 1295, Giovanni remained in Siena and by 1293 he had somehow rid himself and Siena of Ramo di Paganello, who removed to Orvieto on or before that date. In March 1294 Giovanni was a witness to a formal reconciliation between a husband and wife, which may be significant as indicating his journey to France, since both parties were transalpine, the husband, Giovanni di Giovanni, being of French origin and the wife from the north beyond Italy.[5] In December of that year he was a witness to a deed of purchase for a house on ground needed by the Cathedral. In 1295 the *Operaio* of the Pisa Baptistry agreed to pay him a sum of money for work on the Baptistry, but since the sum was not available, a piece of real estate was sold in order to pay him and his workers up to 29 May. In July he received 15 Pisan *soldi* bequeathed to him by one Alcherio di Bonabergo and in the same month apparently quarrelled with the *Operaio* of the Pisan Baptistry, Bonaccorso, concerning an act of proxy. This tantalizing and unexplained difference of opinion, so characteristic of Giovanni's dealings with Cathedral officials, merely adds another touch to the elusive portrait of Giovanni suggested in so many of the surviving documents. Bonaccorso had undertaken to act for Giovanni in his absence for a specific period exactly established as being between 12 June 1289 and 17 February 1303. On 7 July 1295, during or after Giovanni's business trip to Pisa, Bonaccorso renounced the deed, stating that he would no longer involve himself with any affairs arising from it.

Returned from Pisa, Giovanni was appointed to a committee to decide the placing of a fountain. Dispute having arisen, Giovanni and five other masters, including the painter Duccio, together with six citizens, gave judgement in the matter. In December 1295 Giovanni was involved as *capomaestro* in the repairs of the *Bagni di Petriolo*, celebrated for its medicinal waters, and received the significantly high salary of 10 *soldi* per day in accordance with his rank. And finally, in the last Sienese documents of the time relating to Giovanni, he was required to play a part in the construction of a new Sienese Baptistry. He was placed in charge of this project, which took into account the whole area around the Cathedral and involved the purchase and destruction of buildings to enlarge this space. Typically, these plans were frustrated and although the foundations of the Baptistry should have been laid in September 1296, money was not available to purchase the house of one Baldo di Bagnese, so matters were suspended until the next meeting of the Council of the Campana to be held in July 1297. Delays continued; disputes, by implication, mounted. The matter was not resolved until Giovanni had long been gone from Siena.

It will be seen from these revealing if slender archives that the progress on the façade of Siena Cathedral is nowhere detailed, that the *capomaestro* of the building had many external duties, that he was a personage of considerable importance and that he was as beset with business affairs and attendant frustrations as such a man could be, especially one who was not easy to deal with. The ultimate blows fell in 1297 and once more the outcome of the scandal in which Giovanni was involved remains obscure.

For some time the condition of the Cathedral Works had been causing concern. The craftsmen were sufficiently restless for special provision to be made to grant them wine from the Cathedral cellars to prevent them from wasting time elsewhere.[6] In 1296 it was understandably thought desirable to appoint to the *Opera* a good and legal clerk of works, an *Operaio*, who could read and write so that accounts should in future be properly kept. Then in May 1297 a massive investigation was instituted which revealed serious negligence or malpractice in the whole conduct of affairs. Discipline both of masters and men was stated to be wholly lacking. Time, money and materials were said to have been deplorably wasted. Sculpture is described as standing roughed out and abandoned, blackened and covered with lichen, while marble blocks and unfinished carvings lay split and fragmented in the yard. Records as to where worked stones were to be placed were reported lost and detailed plans forgotten. It seemed that no working model could be found. Severe action was taken. A decree was promulgated that the *capomaestro* and all masters past, present, permanent and temporary, should be seized and held 'in chains' upon the spot until matters could be resolved and the work could properly continue on the building. In the event of a failure to achieve results within a month, the governors and defenders of the Commune, and the Mercantile Consuls reserved to themselves the right to take further coercive action against the *capomaestro* and his associates.

Giovanni Pisano is not mentioned by name. If he was held in chains in the Cathedral marble yard, he escaped or was released. If he was *capomaestro*, as everything points to his having been, he must have borne a heavy share of responsibility for the chaos into which the great architectural and sculptural scheme had fallen but there is no absolute evidence that he was still *capomaestro* at the date of the scandal, however strong the presumption may be.

At the beginning of his decade at Siena we have his name without the title: at the end we have the title without his name. All that we know is that he left, or fled from, Siena in 1297, leaving ten years' work upon the most ambitious project of his life in total confusion. No one can explain how so great a master could have been so negligent of the fate of so great an undertaking, nor if the fault lay in the man. No one knows whether he was the loser in some conspiracy of faction, a driven man guilty of malpractices or the innocent victim of the negligence and stupidity or enmity of others. Conceivably he was drawn into the last convulsions of the long and bitter feud between Guelphs and Ghibellines or perhaps there is a simpler explanation in terms of what we should call intolerable bureaucratic incompetence. No protest, no appeal, no confession, no explanation, no word of any sort is known to exist concerning the cruel disorder in which he left, or was forced to leave, the work. We are forced to guess at his architectural intentions in the absence of a model. We do not know the extent to which his architectural intentions were followed and we do not know precisely what they were, but they were abandoned before the completion of the façade, as it now exists, in the 1370's. The unadorned front of the building had been raised in 1264 and thereafter work proceeded fitfully on its decoration.

Ristoro d'Arezzo, the writer, commented with satisfaction on the proposed sculptural decoration as early as 1282 but Giovanni's contribution, even if it were carried out as he intended, cannot have seen the work advanced above the level of the arcades over the lateral doors. Above these, the whole central feature including the insertion of the great *fenestra rotunda*, the financing of which had been discussed as early as 1287, remained unfinished until the 1370's, when it was undertaken in circumstances of economic difficulty increased by the collapse of the Sienese banking houses and in the aftermath of the Black Death.[7] By then Giovanni had been dead for more than fifty years.

If the economies necessitated by these circumstances led to a substantial modification of Giovanni's intentions we can only conceive what they may have been from the existing portal zone, completed during his lifetime, and there is no evidence that he himself either altered an original design for the rest of the façade or was responsible for that original design. All that remains, to suggest that his conception was embedded in the memory of those concerned with the further execution of the façade, is the disposition of the sculpture and the extraordinary and radically new role that sculpture was called upon to play in relation to the architecture. It is enough.

As John White puts it,[8] 'In a typical French Gothic cathedral such as Amiens, the figures tend either to replace main architectural features like the columns in the jambs of the doorways, or else are ranged across the façade like guardsmen, every figure rigidly within the architectural confines of its niche and all of them acting as enriched, but fundamentally architectural features. At Siena, on the contrary, architecture has become a stage, a natural habitat in which cliff-dwelling figures walk and gesture, argue and discuss, crying their prophecies out across the architectural spaces.

'The application of revolutionary principles previously seen in tomb and pulpit to the structure and decoration of a great façade,' he continues, 'is wholly consonant with the attribution of the scheme to a son of Nicola Pisano.'

Full notes to the plates are on page 214

94

95

96

97

98

99

104

105

106

107

108

6 The Siena Cathedral Façade: The Ivories and Wood Carvings

IN SEPTEMBER 1260, thirty-seven years before Giovanni's abrupt departure from the city, the Florentines and their allies marched upon Siena. On the eve of battle, Buonaguida Lucari, to whom the Council had entrusted the defence of the state, assembled the citizens and called upon them to lay themselves, their possessions 'and the whole city of Siena at the feet of the Queen and Empress of Everlasting Life, the glorious and ever virgin Mother of God'. This they did. Next day the Sienese, together with the forces of the Emperor Manfred, crushingly defeated their Guelph opponents at the battle of Montaperto. The victory established an uneasy Ghibelline supremacy in Siena for seventeen years but within half a decade it had begun to crumble. Siena's enlistment of the Virgin's aid did not prevent Manfred from being killed at Benevento in 1266 nor Provenzano Salviani, the commander of the Sienese army in the field, from being defeated at Colle di Val d'Elsa in 1269 and thereafter beheaded. By 1277 the Guelph party had bloodily taken and would hold power in Siena until, like Ghibelline Pisa, the city would fall to Florence and ultimately lose its independence permanently.

This total political reversal no more affected Siena's continuing dedication to the Virgin as 'Governor' of the city than it prevented the Pisan Giovanni from being employed to celebrate the ever-virgin Mother of God on the façade of the Cathedral, and despite the ceaseless and by now impenetrable tangle of complications and interruptions which have largely come to obscure any unity of design, the erection and decoration of the façade continued for over a century.

The scheme of decoration of the façade retains one unifying factor. It is entirely dedicated to the glory of the Virgin, and Giovanni's specifically sculptural contribution to this celebration is centred upon the foreknowledge of the Incarnation believed to have been communicated in antiquity to the prophets and sibyls.

The symbolic interpretation of the New Testament by means of the Old had, by the late thirteenth century, been elaborated into the most minute particulars and, by *interpretatio Christiana*, pagan philosophers and sibyls were admitted to the company of those Old Testament prophets who had foreseen aspects of the Christian miracle. Giovanni intended to show these seers ranged across the façade, each figure not only symbolizing but demonstrating the vital importance of his or her prevision of these greatest of all events.[1] It seems likely that as the work progressed, Giovanni's compulsion to demonstrate the urgency of this communication increased, so that the later sculptures in the sequence are related to one another by their gestures in animated discussion. The stone dialogue increased in energy as it came to be shared between the protagonists so that to the spectator it must have seemed that it was this that brought the prophets and philosophers out into the open to stand poised upon narrow and dangerous ledges high above the ground. These perilous walks were their acting area. They played out their prophetic roles with the whole city of Siena as their auditorium.

In this deliberate staging of a scene, Giovanni's scheme foreshadows those liturgical dramas which by the fifteenth century became famous as *Rappresentazione Sacra*, wherein popular dramatization of themes from the Gospels were performed. But just as any play which depended upon more than the spectacle would become incomprehensible if the script were mislaid during production, so the fact that Giovanni had left Siena without seeing his 'actors' emplaced, and with some of them probably incomplete, prevented him from directing the drama systematically, the more especially since the drama itself was not a simple and popular version of a Gospel story but an abstruse and learned dialogue between remote if powerful intellectuals and visionaries. The disarray of his cast of characters and the inevitable loss of intelligibility may well have been as bitterly painful to him as the turmoil resulting from a staging of *Hamlet* might be to a director who had spent ten years on preparing a production only to know that throughout its long run, it would be performed by amnesiacs. Tragically then, Giovanni's one opportunity to execute an entire scheme of monumental sculpture was abruptly terminated and must be recorded as a failure to achieve that intellectual totality of parts and parts of parts which Thomist theology had deemed the summit of logical exposition. How much this meant to Giovanni as a man and how much he consequently suffered, we can only guess, but from that time forward his art was reduced to the scale of the pulpit. Even if the pulpit itself in the hands of the Pisani had come to constitute a 'cathedral in little', it surely cannot have proved an adequate compensation to one whose enormous energy is manifest even in the smallest detail of his work.

It is obviously as vain to hope to think oneself back into the state of mind of a sculptor so far removed from one in time as Giovanni Pisano, as it is to hope to know how much the meaning, as opposed to the formal achievement, of his sculpture concerned him. I do not think, however, that speculation is wholly without value in the presence of the cobbled and patched-up figures of the Siena façade.

Many people view the sculpture of the past as so many *disjecta membra* to be enjoyed aesthetically without recourse to any troublesome 'meaning' that may have been intended by those who ordered and those who created them. Others perhaps assume that the medieval sculptor was a talented artisan unconcerned with the content of the programme he was forced to follow. I myself believe that to extract from the stone the intensity of expression revealed by Giovanni's sculptures requires the carver to know not only how to do it but what it is he does. I believe he shaped the mouths of his prophets and sibyls to speak the words they uttered. I further believe that the strangely restless spirit of the man, which speaks to us not only through his sculpture but through the dry and tattered curtain of documents which suggest his perturbation by reference to unknown 'crimes', possible peculations, quarrels, rivalries and rejections of authority, is likely to be relevant to his personality and his temperament.

In Siena today the façade of the Cathedral is painstakingly ornamented with lifeless facsimiles of his sculpture whilst the weathered and shattered originals have been removed to the Museum, where they stand in two lines, their prophetic dialogue permanently interrupted. Yet despite this final disjuncture and the tragic condition of many of the individual statues,[2] most of them still speak as few stones have ever spoken. Each passionate monologue, as it has now become, in some degree maintains its urgency. Plato, Isaiah, Solomon, David, Habakkuk, Joshua and Balaam still proclaim the vital consequence of what is to come, and she who has come to be called 'Mary of Moses' still makes her sibylline voice heard, hissing as did her serpentine ancestress, the Pythia of Delphi. The Erythrean Sibyl's lips are shut, her oracle is uttered, but of the others, Moses and Simeon are quiet indeed, recut, restored and renovated into a grey, painted silence. As for the prophet Haggai, the half of him surviving is exiled to London and Aristotle is yet further removed, for although his body stands with his fellows in Siena, his head has been replaced. In the eighteenth century some clownish mechanical made him a new one in the taste of the time and placed it on an incorrect axis, whilst Daniel, if what is left of the trunk of this statue represents Daniel, is exiled to the Cathedral repository, where he lies in a crate. He wears a nineteenth-century head curiously resembling Garibaldi.

When Giovanni left Siena his figures stood in the confusion of the marble yard. Today they stand in careful but no less confused sequence in a museum, interspersed with figures from other parts of the façade by other and lesser sculptors of later date. He did not see them in place on the Cathedral; neither do we. If some remained unfinished when he left, they were doubtless finished only in degree less feebly by his immediate successors than by the ham-handed artisans who in later years botched up his work in 'restoring' it. In his mind's eye he must have seen his prophets jutting from the façade, their shoulders hunched, their heads thrust vigorously outward or twisting to engage their neighbours in debate.

97, 102, 96
99, 105, 100, Cat. 221, 103
Pls. 93, 94

Pls. 95, 98, 104
Pl. 101

Cat. 225

Cat. 216

It has been reasonably supposed that the astonishing formal distortions which Giovanni evolved to enhance the immediacy of the colloquy between certain of his seers and sibyls were intended to 'correct' the optical illusion created for the spectator by his angle of vision from far below, but they were more than that. He shaped the marble into vessels of a superhuman vitality, a vitality inspired to convey the high drama of the event. To do this was to release from the stone not only the figure but the piercing voice of which each was only the instrument. To say that the head of Haggai is that of 'a thirteenth-century Laocoön'[3] is to come far nearer to understanding Giovanni's Dionysiac classicism than any comparison with 'the bland statuary of Reims', but Giovanni's tight control of *contraposto* invariably prevents the histrionic gesticulation to be found in the Laocoön itself which disperses its energy in vain rhetoric. His sculpture springs but the spring is tightly coiled.

Giovanni's use of the drill to give 'colour' and change of texture to the surface of his sculpture has its counterpart in Hellenistic carving. By abrupt and deep undercutting and by the device of linked drill holes, his unique calligraphy emphasizes those sudden shifts from light to dark which make Pope-Hennessy's use of the term 'like brush-strokes' tally with Moore's metaphor of the claw tool as a 'paintbrush' in the hand of Michelangelo.

In a state of exhilarating and contagious excitement when first confronted with the Siena figures, Moore proposed that we should give a whole chapter of this book to Giovanni's carving of the human mouth and I realized that it was precisely this vital detail which, twenty years earlier, had captured my own imagination, for the mouth seems to me to have been to Giovanni what the muscles of the torso were to Michelangelo – the seat of expression.

Art-historians have drawn attention to Nicola's predilection for the 'Byzantine' open mouth and have also cited precedents for it in the sculpture of Dietrich (or Dietmar) and Sizzo in the statues of the choir of Naumburg Cathedral.[4] Be that as it may, no other sculpture is so trumpet-tongued. Although much defaced by weather, some of the words the Sibyls and Prophets spoke are incised upon their scrolls or upon the façade (where fortunately for us they determine the originally intended position of each figure) but when Balaam cries *Orietur stella ex Jacob* or Isaiah proclaims *Ecce Virgo concipiet et pariet filium* the lapidary words seem to burst from between the stone lips of the Prophets, as Mary's sharply indrawn breath at the moment she receives the Annunciation can be 'heard' in the marble at Pisa. That this sharp breath should thus be shown in sculpture at this time is by no means *Pls. 69, 70* unrelated to the words spoken by Buonaguida Lucari of Siena, on the eve of battle.

When Siena, on that decisive day in 1260, gave not only all its people and all their goods, but the very city itself into the Virgin's possession and when that city in gratitude began to build the most elaborate cathedral façade ever conceived in Italy, wholly to be dedicated to the exposition of her glory, then Mary's divine role in temporal affairs had achieved a new dimension in Tuscany. It was not new in Europe, for the cult had been growing since the twelfth century, but it was a visible sign that a new balance between the male and female roles had been needed and had been evolved.

The most influential factor in this process was the proliferation both in manuscript and by word of mouth of the *Legenda Aurea*, a book written between 1263 and 1288 by the Dominican Jacobus de Voragine. He was not alone among ecclesiastical writers who expanded the brief references in the Gospels to those who had played their parts in the life of Christ, adding domestic and human details to the story in the form of Apocryphal Gospels, but it was the *Legenda Aurea* which became the main source of the personal legend of the life of the Virgin. In it the joys and sorrows of Mary are described much as if she were a contemporary and in the golden light of this legend she became as familiar in her humanity as any thirteenth-century housewife upon whom an incredible role had been thrust.

However darkly, through the glass of the human condition, the physical world reflected the divine, the human need to see the one in the other had become demandingly present to ordinary men and women. Giovanni was a man if not an ordinary one. What did Mary mean to him? Surely it cannot have been solely that her cult and her increasing accessibility as a mediatrix made her image more viable as an artefact. Was it that her release from hieratic aloofness enabled Giovanni and his contemporaries in France and elsewhere to incorporate their personal observation of the female sex within the established schemata of their image-making? Or was it an exploration of the special nature of the relationship between mother and child which he himself had experienced as father or as son which give his Madonna groups their radiant gravity?

We do not know, at a human level, whom Giovanni loved. We probably never shall. We do know, surely, how deeply he loved and with what poetry both in religious and human terms he expressed his love, for we have the evidence of the Madonnas which stud his career like stars in a crown. This being so, surely a great complex of sculptures ranged across a cathedral façade and centrally concerned with the Incarnation and with the Virgin possessed greater emotional significance to Giovanni than the learned manipulation of symbols, although these in turn must have meant more intellectually to him than they may do to us. If, with a great effort, one strives to cast one's mind into a medieval mould and so interpret a group of carved stones at several levels of meaning, one may as well add the humane, for it is the passionate humanity of Giovanni with its flaws and eccentricities which pierces the curtain of time and separates him, once and for all, from the anonymity which convention has imposed upon the medieval craftsman. It is this which makes him the true forerunner of the Renaissance.

Whatever one may personally consider Giovanni's special contribution to the cult of the Virgin may have been, that cult was intense and general during his lifetime, and the extent to which Mary could become identified with womanhood may not only be seen in the increasingly intimate and charming representations of her in French cathedral sculpture but in the poetry written to her. This, in France, bore a striking resemblance, however contradictory, to the hedonistic verses of courtly love, so that she came to be imagined at once as the Mother of God, whose coronation as Queen of

Heaven raised her to a supreme elevation, and as Our Lady, a term of reverent familiarity which made her accessible to the most grievous sinners as one who, being a woman, might be expected to intercede for them with special tenderness. This element of empathy, of personal identification with the divine in human guise in imagery, would of course lead in time to violent iconoclasm but Aquinas himself gave sanction to this apparent idolatry when he wrote in the *Summa Theologica* that 'the same reverence should be paid to the image of Christ as to Christ Himself. Since therefore Christ ought to be worshipped with the adoration of *latria* (i.e. the adoration paid to God) it follows that His image should also be worshipped with the adoration of *latria*'[5] and he backs his words by citing the painting of the Virgin by St Luke 'which is kept in Rome'. Nor was it only in visual images that empathy was manifest. The Virgin's family background, her affectionate relationship with her parents which may be seen recorded in Giotto's frescoes at Padua or Tino's relief on the Siena Cathedral façade, were set forth in prose and verse for those who could read, and read by those who painted and carved.

The Son of God who stared into His own destiny from His Mother's lap turns towards her without losing divinity and they are united as Mother and Child.[6] The release contained in this movement is as much an epitome of empathy as the image of Christ suffering upon the cross. Its importance to painting and sculpture lies in the fact that once the Child has turned He is free to suckle, to play with goldfinches or even to dislodge a grape pip from between His milk teeth, as He does in Masaccio's 'Pisa' Madonna. He can still turn back towards the spectator and contemplate all suffering humanity, but He has shown Himself to be a child.

To this physical movement Giovanni gave a special and gentle twist and in one instance the form of it has created an enigma. The Madonna and Child carved for the tympanum of the door of the Pisa Baptistry shows the Child seeming to bless those who enter the building. He faces forward and ignores the penetrating glance his Mother brings to bear on Him. It may be seen as a significant movement[7] but as we see the statue in the Campo Santo today, the Child's head gives the appearance of being recut and is disproportionately small. The gesture of the right hand seems indecisive and although the marble is now so grimed as to forbid close examination, the work gives the appearance of being yet another victim of false 'restoration'. The Child's feet are both missing and the head has clearly been broken off and replaced. It is my opinion that originally the Christ Child returned His Mother's glance and at some subsequent date the head of the figure was reorientated.

This Madonna group has been dated between 1295 when Giovanni briefly visited Pisa from Siena and 1300 when he had been gone from Siena for three years. In December 1297 he signed a contract with the Pisa Cathedral authorities, which covered his rent and referred to him merely as *magister lapidorum* rather than *caput magistrorum*. Whether he left Siena in disgrace as a result of the scandal in the marble yard or had done so voluntarily, having been cleared of guilt, is not known. He maintained his Sienese citizenship and his tax immunities which argues for the latter case, and he was not deprived of the property he had acquired there.

Pls. 64–66

Fig. t

Pls. 119, 120

CRUCIFIXES
111   Wooden crucifix. Siena. Museo dell'Opera del Duomo
112   Fragment of boxwood crucifix. Staatliche Museen, Berlin-Dahlem
113   Wooden crucifix. Pistoia. Church of S. Andrea
114/5   Fragment of ivory crucifix. London. Victoria and Albert Museum

Full notes to the plates are on page 218

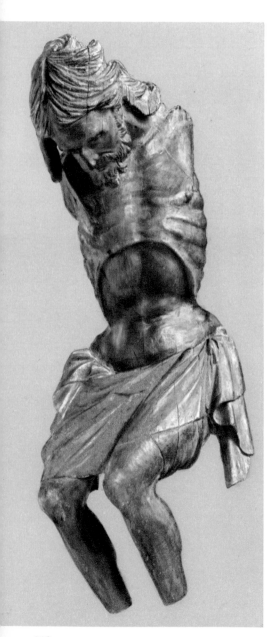

112

113

116

117

Between the termination of his work in Siena and the completion of his next major work,

Pls. 124–154 the pulpit for S. Andrea at Pistoia, he produced or supervised the production of a formidable quantity of work in various media. His difficult temperament was again in evidence and whether from over-work or an incapacity to organize, which may have contributed to the Siena debacle, he came once more into conflict with authority. In June 1298 he was ordered by the Pisa Cathedral authorities to complete a work in ivory by Christmas on pain of a heavy fine. 'The categorical terms in which this caution is couched,' as Pope-Hennessy[8] says, 'leave no doubt that this work was of considerable consequence.' It was an ivory 'table' with statuettes for the high altar. If the two surviving works in

Pls. 116, 117 ivory attributed to Giovanni are portions of this work, the larger is the Madonna and Child now in the Museo San Matteo, and like so many of Giovanni's works, she has suffered cruelly. The repairs to which this group has been subjected between 1433 and 1933 are documented and it is clear that the Child has been reorientated in relation to the Mother much as, I have suggested, is the case with the marble group for the Baptistry door. The head was originally turned towards the Mother, whilst the right hand was raised in a benediction presumably more convincing than the vague gesture the marble figure now makes. It has been claimed that the Child's head is either seventeenth-century[9] or nineteenth-century,[10] whilst the orb which the false right hand holds was specious even before it was stolen and replaced in 1933. It may be that there is a closer relationship in adversity between the ivory and the marble than has been remarked.

Of the 'table' of ivory described in the original contract as *Tabulam unam eburneam ab altari maiori cum ymaginibus*,[11] a description exists dating from 1433, when the work first required renovation, which describes it as having a tabernacle at the centre with the Virgin and Child and two angels wearing metal wings, the latter an indication of Giovanni's activity as a goldsmith, all examples of which are lost. In addition, there were three further figures in ivory and two Passion scenes. Of

Pls. 114, 115 these various elements of the whole, nothing was known, after the sixteenth century, until the ivory of the Crucified Christ was discovered by Pope-Hennessy, who has convincingly suggested that this may have been part of one of the Passion scenes.

The Madonna and Child, for all her repairs, remains a majestic creation. Giovanni took full and beautiful advantage of the natural curve of the long length of tusk to show the Virgin in that 'pregnant' pose so long lasting in fashion that the Elizabethan poet Thomas Nashe could praise a woman who assumed it as 'bearing out her belly as magestical as an estrich'. Her pelvis is thrust forward in this fashionable stance and turned to carry, on her left hip, the agreeable burden of the Child. She is at once gay, grave and majestical in her spiralling movement and nothing short of the total destruction she so nearly suffered in the Cathedral fire of 1595 could deprive her of these qualities. In the Madonna for the tomb of Margaret of Luxembourg, of Giovanni's last phase, a figure stripped by almost as much destruction as stone can sustain, the same organic movement remains, though head, child and left arm are missing. All particulars are lost. What remains are weight, grace and energy.

116/7   Ivory Madonna and Child.
       Pisa. Museo San Matteo

To adapt the curve of an elephant's tusk to the pose of a draped female figure is not in itself especially remarkable. It is a commonplace of both French Gothic and oriental ivory carving. What is remarkable in Giovanni's ivory is the secondary curve, the *contraposto* he has contrived to give the figure within the larger form of the tusk. It is this which gives the figure such pride and such vitality, for, in carving, it is *contraposto* that releases the latent energy of forms from their matrix, whether it be stone, wood or ivory.

Perhaps the most consequential milestones in the whole history of sculpture come, in a double sense, at turning points. At the moment when, as the sixth century BC turned into the fifth, some unknown Attic sculptor turned the *kouros* (whose rigid and frontal pose had been maintained for centuries in Egypt before he entered Greece), pivoting him on one hip and redistributing his weight so that hips and shoulders move counter to each other – at this transcendental moment the figure moved in the stone and won the freedom to swing upon its axis, as a man may turn in nature to address the companion who stands beside him. This movement became necessary to sculpture when narrative came to play an increasingly important role in the visual arts, for how, without this *contraposto*, can the participants in an event be convincingly related to one another? It lost its impetus when the Western Empire of Rome broke up and imagery ossified once more to bear the weight of Byzantium. Then in the crucial period when 'worship by empathy' captured the minds and hearts of Christians, the hieratic once more gave way to the humane, for who can identify in humane terms with gods or sacred persons who cannot or need not move? And in the springing movement of the thirteenth century, sculpture turned once more. The word 'spring', like the word 'turn', may be as readily applied to seasons as to actions. No master of this turn, this 'dramatic twist' of forms moving counter to one another within the limber architecture of the human frame, surpassed Giovanni Pisano in medieval art. The spring he gave the stone contains the Spring of the Renaissance itself.

The only other surviving ivory by Giovanni is the mutilated figure of Christ Crucified which *Pls. 114, 115* may be a fragment of one of the two Passion scenes from the 'table with images' made for Pisa Cathedral. The characteristic elements of style to which Pope-Hennessy draws attention[12] in his comparison of this figure with the Crucifixion panels at Pistoia and Pisa and the three Crucifixes in wood at Pistoia, Siena and Berlin are convincingly present, especially in Giovanni's unusually sharp *Pls. 111, 112, 113* definition of the lower edge of the rib cage, a personal characteristic of his style equally marked in the Hercules of the Pisa pulpit, the only fully nude male figure in Giovanni's canon. *Pl. 170*

The ivory differs from Giovanni's other crucifixions in that the figure has passed beyond pain. *Pls. 141, 164* Both the marbles show Christ strung in the final agony, every tendon and sinew at full stretch, the abdomen drawn in under the rib cage with the pain of drawing breath. At Siena, the wooden figure on its knotted tree twists, the legs turn counter to the chest, whilst in the Pistoia crucifix they pull upwards to take the weight from the nail. In each the arms are wrenched upwards on taut ligaments as the pelvis drags down from the started ribs. Cramp was the torment of the cross and it is cramp that Giovanni shows in wood. By contrast the Christ in ivory is relaxed. He is gone into death, the marks of the long agony are left upon the figure, but they no longer contort it. His eyes are closed. The moment of release seems to hold him suspended, weightless. Even the missing arms, which show themselves only in the mind's eye, are relaxed, unstrung, and to judge from the angle of their jointure to the figure were not wrenched upwards. The cage of rib no longer gasps to hold in the breath. An unearthly moment is witnessed, a split second, in which the soul's rise buoys up the worn cage of the body and neither the slow slump of man into clay, nor his hardening into rigor mortis has begun.

Because in the twentieth century sculpture has in general rejected narrative, we no longer seek particularities of time in sculpture but rather generalizations of form. The moment beyond life, the instant beyond the whispered *Consummatum Est*, has rarely been so marvellously made permanent and that peace-filled smoothing of the features in death which has so often been described in literature, represents a brief span of time made timeless by the cognition of form and no less by the comprehension of the material, by the nature of ivory.

During the thirteenth century, the representations in painting and in sculpture of Christ Crucified show, with increasing emphasis, the extremity of the physical suffering endured upon the cross. In the north, particularly in the Rhineland, this torment is terrible indeed. It is a trend which runs parallel, both north and south of the Alps, with the increasingly gay and intimate relationship which the Christ Child enjoys with His Mother as He moves in her arms.

It may be that some deep identification existed for the sculptor between the cross as a wooden structure and the god who hung upon it, for it is often in wood that these crucifixions plumb the greatest depths of empathy. Wood is an organic substance with its own determined form of growth; the conjunction of limb to trunk is not merely a verbal synonym and perhaps in some sort the crucifix is buried in the windy tree as the crucified is buried in the cross.

Both wood and stone can of course be contrived to imitate almost any effect. They can be made to counterfeit each other as they in turn can be copied in metal, but the inorganic structure of stone is a determinant which remains, unless it is falsified, wholly different from the gesticulating olive or the painful thornbush. That these barriers should be crossed and recrossed to the detriment of the material in sculpture does not alter the fact.

Ivory is also an organic substance which makes specific demands and grants specific rewards in its use. It was, in the Middle Ages, a rare and precious material but one for which the demand grew so great that vanity and technical skill combined to induce its carvers to indulge in florid if sometimes charming display. The specific qualities of ivory, its density of grain and response to precision invite both suppleness of form and sharpness of contour. It can sustain minute particularity of detail which can topple a work all too readily into trivial elaboration or blandness of surface. Giovanni escaped these temptations, never losing the largeness of his forms nor exploiting the smoothness of ivory for its own sake. In the ivory crucifix, the abrupt opposition of the heavy and deeply cut folds of the loincloth to the light and slender torso marks the edge of pain. It is as if the cloth were stiff where pain had lodged as it drained from the body.

In his woodcarving, Giovanni seems to have been unique in the Italy of his time. Repaying his debt to France for gentle influences received, he has left us sculpture which, though blunted now by ugly overpaint, yet holds the power to blast the roots of trees. It is not that their gestures are extravagant nor their forms so emaciated that, like many North Alpine crucifixes, they protest their torment to the edge of the grotesque, but rather that they enclose their formal tension without protest. In the ivory even the rhetoric of the tree is gone but the contained power is worthy of the bearer of the tusk from which it came.

Full notes to the plates are on page 220

119

120

121

122

7 *The Return to Pisa and the Pistoia Pulpit*

IN THE YEARS following his departure from Siena, the burden of work which Giovanni undertook for Pisa and Pistoia may well have been too great. There is a stage in an artist's life when he cannot afford either to reject or to accept commissions and when he stands in the public regard too high in reputation to lack creative opportunities but is too pressed to work at them in peace. Not only was he to be in trouble over the delay in completing the ivory *tabula* and at full stretch on the carvings to be assembled into the pulpit of Pistoia but, if Vasari is to be even in part believed, he was overwhelmed with tasks the results of which are lost. His civic duties at Pisa included taking soundings of the Leaning Tower with rope and lead, inside and outside, in the presence of a notary, presumably with a view to establishing and if possible obviating its further rate of slant. At this time he is referred to only as *magister lapidorum*, but by April 1298 he comes once more to be called *Capomaestro*, and there is evidence that further work on the Tower was undertaken in 1301 and 1302 when it would seem he planned to make a provisional wooden frame for the top of the Tower which would later be overlaid with marble. Since the full height of the Tower as it stands today was not attained during Giovanni's lifetime, it is impossible to tell what work he actually carried out on the structure.

Pls. 119, 120
Pls. 80–91 As a sculptor he was once more employed on the exterior decoration of the Baptistry and, apart from carving the Madonna for the tympanum of the principal door, he worked with his assistants on the freestanding figures which surmounted the pinnacles of the tabernacles containing the colossal half-length figures which he had carved in some degree of collaboration with his father thirteen years earlier.

Certain of the Siena sculptures, notably the Erythraean Sibyl, the Plato and the Habakkuk, are related in style not only to the colossal figures for the Pisa Baptistry but also to the high reliefs on the Perugia Fountain. In the 'Mary Sister of Moses', however, he had achieved an extreme tension or *contraposto* which the deep niches containing the colossi could not begin to contain. This great turning movement he now developed in two of the pinnacle figures.

Both represent women wearing voluminous skirts which they manipulate with such grace that in the Pisa Museum one of them is described as 'dancing'. She is certainly in movement but *Pls. 83, 84* since her head is missing and her feet are invisible it is, I suspect, the plasticity and swing of her ample drapery which has earned her this description. The other sculpture of equal splendour is complete and motionless but her pose is one of stillness poised between two actions. Grasping her long skirt *Pls. 80–82* in both hands she has pulled it taut across her body below the breasts whilst she stoops her head and shoulders forward. What she is doing is listening intently. Eyes narrowed, head at a slight tilt, she is waiting tensely to hear words which can come to her only from the sky. No 'optical correction', designed to 'correct' a figure when made to be seen from below, explains the true nature of the pose. It derives from the need to convey urgency and the urgency is of one who waits breathless to receive communication. She waits, as I suspect her sister 'dancing' figure moved restlessly, to hear, and she pins her elbows back against her sides in her anxiety. She is wound up like a crossbow, as if the bolt, were it released, would pierce armour. The principle of axiality is here used to coil energy inside the stone and Giovanni takes great liberties with the human form to do it. The power controlled by the interlocking of the forms is held in tension by the fact that from any point of view, including those from which it could never have been viewed in Giovanni's day, the tensions coil and transpose towards the centre of the stone.

Six other figures which once crowned the pinnacles above the Baptistry niches possess this *Pls. 85–91, Cat. 210* formal tension in varying degrees. The workshop figures which stand today in the same rooms of the museum are as remote from them as clay from tempered steel. As with much medieval art the participation of workshop assistants, sometimes of scant talent, stands cheek by jowl with the work of masters. It may be readily explained on such practical grounds as pressure of work upon the master, but it is not easy to understand unless it is assumed that the message, the meaning of every work, far surpassed in importance the execution of its parts – and this does not wholly convince. In Giovanni's case overwhelming pressure of work seems more probable. In the fifteen years between his departure from Siena and the completion of the Pisa Cathedral pulpit, this pressure must have become insupportable. With the four years of work for the Pistoia pulpit between 1297 and 1301 he allowed nothing to interfere, or alternatively he subjected all other projects to it. It is the most perfectly preserved of all his major works and it is the most faultless. Since it was apparently received without adverse criticism and subject to no financial dispute, and since it would have been compared with his father's achievements and with those of Giovanni's greatest contemporary, Arnolfo di Cambio, it must have been considered a masterpiece, and in the neatly rhymed inscription carved on the pulpit,

Giovanni does not stint himself of praise. It reads:

LAUDE DEI TRINI REM CEPTAM COPULO FINI

CURE PRESENTIS SUB PRIMO MILLE TRICENTIS.

PRINCEPS EST OPERIS PLEBANUS VEL DATOR ERIS

ARNOLDUS DICTUS, QUI SEMPER SIT BENEDICTUS.

ANDREAS UNUS VITELLI . . . QUOQUE TINUS

NATUS VITALI, BENE NOTUS NOMINA TALI,

DISEMSATORES HI DICTI SUNT MELIORES.

SCULPSIT JOHANNES, QUI RES NON EGIT INANES,

NICOLI NATUS SENSIA (SCIENTIA) MELIORE BEATUS,

QUEM GENUIT PISA, DOCTUM SUPER OMNIA VISA.

(In praise of the threefold god, I link the end with the beginning of this task in one thousand three hundred and one. The chief director and donor of the work is Arnoldus the canon, be he ever blessed. Andreas Vitelli . . . also Tino son of Vitale, well known under such a name, are best of treasurers. Giovanni carved it who performed no empty works. Born of Nicola, but blessed with greater science, Pisa gave him birth and endowed him with learning in visual things.)

It is a boast, and in the light of the work itself, it is a justified one. Despite the vigour and ferocity of parts of it and the tenderness and delicacy of others it is a *summa* in stone wherein all parts and parts of parts coalesce to form a harmonious whole. In its particulars it is all that the sophisticated Thomist could have required, and if a less informed although no less pious laity elected to interpret Giovanni's imagery at a visionary level rather than in a didactic way, that would depend upon whose voice rang from the pulpit and whose finger pointed to the appropriate image to strengthen his sermon. The iconographic scheme of both Nicola's earlier pulpits, the first at Pisa and the second at Siena, upon which, under Nicola's tutelage, Giovanni had cut his sculptor's teeth, is closely followed at Pistoia. Giovanni would have seen the former daily as he worked once again on the Baptistry façade, just as he had seen the latter daily during his sojourn at Siena. His primary innovation in the narrative panels at Pistoia is the organization of the space wherein his protagonists play out the sacred drama. Where Nicola packed his figures together, ordering their forms first with a stern Roman gravity and later with a Gothic complexity, Giovanni not only gives them larger room to act but greater depth to breathe in. He shows them behaving physically and psychologically as those who contemplate the sculpture would themselves expect to behave. And so compelling is the identification to be made that the astonishing distortions of the human frame he invented are apparent only when, by disengaging from the drama, the mind can be brought to bear on the formal elements.

Pl. 140 The Massacre of the Innocents is carved with relentless brutality. Its brutality must have bludgeoned response from the brutalized, from those who all too frequently had watched but escaped the common savagery following the sack of a medieval town. Terror is hacked into the stone so that the forms of dead and doomed children seem bloat and thick and their mothers suffer the sculptor's hammer blows, beating them into anguished submission. In the foreground three motionless, stricken women grasp their murdered children. The whole centre strains to the left as those who seek to save their newborn retreat in turmoil from the killers, only to be turned and halted below the rigid figure of a soldier who, holding an infant by its legs to butcher it, stands poised above the beastly tumult as motionless as Herod opposite. Grief freezes the women who stand near him but, like a rising tide of protest, men and women thrust upwards against the stream to remonstrate with the king. And Herod himself is a figure of extraordinary ambiguity. The gesture he makes with his right arm appears at first glance to be one of command, an instigation to murder, and in the dim light of the church his face from one angle conveys that disgusted disdain which rulers must often wear when they order necessary atrocities. Viewed from a different angle he wears an expression of horror, and what seems the commanding hand so clutches the edge of his robe *that his next action must be to cover his face*.

Pls. 137–138

Pl. 139

The marks of the chisel are left raw. No smoothing abrasives have polished the surface of this carnage, and the chisels that cut it were sharp. That they were sharp enough to slice into the marble like swords into flesh marks a new tempering of steel. And whilst the pulpit itself was being completed, assembled and erected, newly tempered steel cut into the flesh of the parishioners of S. Andrea. In 1296, civil war broke out between the Black and the White factions of the Guelph party in Pistoia and continued mercilessly during the whole period of Giovanni's work for the city. So great was the violence that special officers called the *Posati* were appointed and Pistoia delivered herself into the power of Florence to restore order. This failed. The war spread to Florence until, in January 1302, the Blacks won so complete a victory that the White leaders fled. One of those to fly from Florence was Dante Alighieri.[1] Those who heard the mendicant preachers call for order and strict observance under the threat of damnation, or their call for poverty, humility and suffering in the name of 'poor Christ', as St Francis had described Him, saw damnation and suffering more dreadfully demonstrated on this panel of Giovanni's pulpit than ever they had seen before in sculpture. They also saw, in the panel of the Annunciation, Nativity and Annunciation to the Shepherds, those homely matters exemplified as when a mother carefully and solicitously arranges a cloak around her child, or a maidservant, holding a nervous and rather unwilling infant, feels the temperature of his bathwater. No longer, as in Nicola's Pisa pulpit, does the Virgin stare with antique austerity into the distance, she copes with the baby. No longer is the Christ Child ritually laved, He kicks against the cradling hand, and, like the rest of this panel, He is carved with exquisite delicacy.

Notes on page 204

Pls. 131–134

The turn of the thirteenth–fourteenth centuries was a time of critical doubt when, to rich and poor alike, salvation outweighed security and salvation was not secure. The aspirations of the poor could be embraced only by religion. To them the Franciscan ideals were but given norms with which they could identify, even if they could not escape them. Paradoxically, while the Church stood more secure in power with the Ghibelline party destroyed, her temporal preoccupations bred their own distrust. The Spirituals with their rejection of all wealth, including that of the Church itself, were locked in a losing struggle not only with the Dominicans who, once the doctrines of Aquinas were officially incorporated in Dominican teaching, represented the official stance of the Church in the matter of temporal power, but with the Conventual moderates of their own Order. An excessive indulgence in the Christian virtue of poverty, and the challenging argument that the Church itself should reject wealth and temporal power, would bring many Spirituals to expulsion, exile and even torture. Meanwhile the Franciscan moderates moved steadily away from their founder's creed as the wealth of the Franciscan Order itself increased. The other and older Orders were less vociferous, but as it became clear that the heroic phase of Franciscan idealism was passing, the stability of medieval society was shaken and that unrest which reached its climax in the aftermath of the Black Death of 1348–49 was already stirring. The Church held on its rock but the waves breaking on it were not stilled.[2]

It is impossible to understand the significance of Nicola's and Giovanni's pulpits unless we think of them as the rostra from which these vital matters were propounded and contested. True, such arguments were heard in every pulpit, but consider the unlikely event of a modern parallel. It would mean not that the opposed orators of our day would make their cases on television or in the press, but that the moral and physical fate of the world would be argued out in a context of the greatest art of our time. Nor would this art be decorative: its meaning would be seen and in different degrees understood by every viewer as absolutely relevant to the debate itself. And consider the beliefs and consciences of the sculptors who created the setting. We know little about them, beyond their work, but they were sentient and intelligent human beings caught up in those webs of anger, compassion, fear, hope and frustation in which we ourselves are entangled. However disparate the views expressed by those who preached, the pulpits by Nicola and Giovanni from which they did so were the outward and visible signs of the core of the faith itself, the visible fountainhead. Before the complexity of these great pulpits, part to part and to the whole, in the multiplicity of meanings interrelating, the formula of Gregory the Great, *protura et ornamenta in ecclesia sunt lectiones et scriptura* becomes inadequate. To the learned they were the book given a simultaneity which the written word could not achieve, and to the lay a discourse given an actuality which the word could not wholly supply. As the Christian legend came to be expanded, so the visible symbols acquired an increased density in elaboration so that a *summa* in stone stood forth and meaning flowed from the corporeal entity of the pulpit as fountain.

Within the still compact entity of the pulpit form, the transformation is vast, for, within those strict limitations of scale, the narrative and symbolism had still to be as readable, to be comprehensible, as a large fresco cycle. So long as the event portrayed was familiar and isolated from its neighbour it could be and had been represented with the simplicity of a Guido da Como, who showed, on his pulpit at S. Bartolommeo in Pantano at Pistoia, the Annunciation on one panel, the Nativity on another and the Adoration of the Magi on a third. A thin trickle from the fountain, these events are shown with touching simplicity in shallow depth and with no evident link between them beyond the universally known fact that these events did occur in sequence. Giovanni, in S. Andrea in the same city, pours forth these events together with the Annunciation to the Shepherds, the Dream of the Magi and the Warning to the Magi composed within two neighbour panels, all parts of which relate formally in the sculpture as well as sequentially to the narrative. Furthermore, the elaboration of particulars is expanded, within the lateral space and depth of the panel, in a fusion of the illusory and the actual. The complexity of this type of composition, instigated by Nicola, made one further dimension imperative, that of time. The establishment of the unities of time and place are as necessary to such an elaboration of particulars as they have always been to narrative produced as drama on the stage. Until Nicola and Giovanni carved their pulpits these unities had not been essential.

Fig. d

Pls. 134, 135

Our recognition of the passage of time is largely based, in the twentieth century, upon our interest in history, believing as we do that historical studies may extend our knowledge of individuals and of peoples and thence our knowledge of ourselves. To medieval man history was of value primarily as it bore upon salvation. Aside from the Testaments, the writings of the Fathers and the persons with whom their works were concerned, the historical individuals of cardinal interest were those whose villainy was sufficiently grandiose and memorable to provide grim example of ensured damnation, those whose philosophy could be incorporated in Christian ethic or, more important, those gifted with the power to foretell in part the coming miracle of Christianity itself.

The prophets were, above all, the figures from the Old Testament whose lives and utterances had a direct bearing on the New and their images constantly feature in medieval sculpture. But as Edgar Wind recounts in his valuable essay on Michelangelo's Prophets and Sibyls:[3] 'While the prophets were appointed to preach to the Jews, the sibyls prophesied to the Gentiles. Together they foreshadow the division of the Church into *Ecclesia Iudaeorum* and *Ecclesia Gentilium*, a distinction suggested by Christ himself when he instructed the disciples, before his death, to teach the new gospel only to the Jews, but urged them later, after his resurrection, to spread the good tidings to all nations.' This distinction between the prophets and their pagan female counterparts is important not only because the sibyls were inserted into Christian theology by the device of *interpretatio Christiana*, as were certain pagan philosophers, but because sibyls were uninstructed in Mosaic law and prophesied without preparation, intuitively.

The sibyl, evidently an image of great importance to Giovanni, was not a common subject in early medieval sculpture and did not widely kindle the poetic imagination until the early Renaissance, when she became fascinating enough to inspire much learned discourse. In antique legend her name derives from a mantic female called Sibylla of Marpessus, of whom a Heracleitan fragment preserved by Plutarch recounts that 'with her maddened mouth . . . she reaches a thousand years with her voice by the power of the god'. Claimed equally by the Erythraeans, she would seem to be the archetypal sibyl but some general confusion not only identified her with her Cumaean rival but with a proliferation of other prophetic females. In the second century AD, Lactantius, who took his list of ten sibyls from Varro's now lost *Antiquitates Rerum Divinarum*, quotes from their prophecies and St Augustine followed Lactantius with particular reference to the Erythraean Sibyl in his *De Civitate Dei*.[4] The Sibylline Books, of which the Sibyl of Cumae was the supposed author, were kept in the Temple of Jupiter Capitolinus and consulted by the Roman senate in times of trouble until they were destroyed by fire in 82 BC, but these were imitated in a collection of apocryphal writings by the Jews and later by the Christians, composed in Greek hexameters. It is these latter apocrypha which gave rise to the Christian sibylline tradition and to the proliferation of Sibyls which occurs in Tuscan sculpture first with Nicola, who has three on the Siena pulpit,[5] and then in the sculpture of Giovanni, who placed six of them on the angles of the archivolt in his Pistoia pulpit and whose workshop was responsible for ten on the Pisa Cathedral pulpit, of which only five survive.

The seemingly indeterminate number of sibyls is the more surprising in view of the medieval passion for symmetrical numbers. This balance, which expressed a belief in a secret harmony between the 'truths' of nature and history, played 'a capital role in the reduction of the diversity of the universe to unity',[6] and as such is continually evident in the sculptural schemata of both Nicola's and Giovanni's programmes. I have already remarked the groups of four Rivers of Paradise, four Elements and four Evangelists, but to these may be added, among others, the seven Capital Sins balanced by seven Cardinal Virtues, seven Celestial Spheres and seven Gifts of the Holy Spirit, twelve Prophets and twelve Apostles, nine Muses and nine Worthies. The list is considerable.[7]

The division of the gift of the Church between Jews and Gentiles, which Wind shows to have been of central importance to the liturgy of the Sistine Chapel and hence to Michelangelo, did not occur to Aquinas as of sibylline inspiration, although he wrote of them as chosen by God to speak *ex inspiratione divina* in the *Summa Theologica*. It is also clear that Nicola Pisano was by no means as interested in the role of the sibyl as was his son. The Renaissance fascination with the subject lay far in the future.

Some digression is justifiable here because sibyls were clearly more significant to Giovanni than to any of his contemporaries and in this he was a Renaissance forerunner in iconography. So confused is the whole identification of sibyls in medieval art that although no less than eighteen hundred lines of the so-called 'Oracles' occur in patristic writings,[8] vast differences of opinion seem to have existed as to who, among a number of sibyls, uttered them. What is paramount in the relationship between the sibyl and the Christian faith is the proposition that the Advent of Christ was foretold by one or more sibyls. The original legend, in Christian terms, apparently originated with, or was first recorded by, Pope Innocent III, and in popular form has come down to us in *The Golden Legend*.[9] But long before the thirteenth century various extraordinary fables about the sibyls had arisen, such as the ninth-century legend that the King and Prophet David was possessed of such a vast 'strength' that it oozed daily and he had a servant to clean the overplus from his 'phial'. This servant wiped the 'strength' off on a patch of grass whereupon a goose ate the grass and laid an egg from which the Sibyl was born.[10]

This tribute to David's virility serves to associate Prophet and Sibyl unusually closely and it is one of many which relate, if less intimately, pagan sibyls to Hebrew prophets, especially Moses, Isaiah, Daniel, David and Solomon and to 'wise pagans', notably Plato; those in fact who are associated with the mantic women portrayed on the façade of Siena Cathedral.

At this point an apocryphal writing, the *Exposito Sibylla et Merlino* falsely attributed to Joachim da Fiore, seems to become especially relevant to the period at which Giovanni was at work, for the story in this form was inspired by the Spirituals and is mentioned by Arnold of Villanova both in 1295 and in 1316 in the appropriately named *Historia Tribulationis*. The predictions fathered upon Joachim, which are specially sibylline, were those of the Erythraean Sibyl as communicated to St Cyril of Constantinople, whilst he was saying Mass, through the intermediary of an angel appearing in a cloud, rather as Giovanni's angels whisper to his sibyls on the Pistoia and Pisa pulpits. These predictions began to gain general currency in 1254 at exactly the time that the notoriously Joachimite Minister General of the Franciscan Order John of Parma relinquished his office to S. Bonaventura and Gerard da Borgo S. Donnino published his subsequently condemned edition of Joachim's collected books, known thereafter as the *Everlasting Gospel*. That these oracles were messianic was already indicated by Bernard de Morval.

In the Requiem Mass, the first verse of the *Dies Irae* describes the Day of Wrath as foretold by David and 'the Sibyl'. *Dies irae, dies illa | solvet saeculum in favilla | teste David cum Sibylla.* The poem itself is now generally accepted as the work of the Franciscan Tomaso di Celano, the biographer of St Francis.[11] It is the greatest hymn on the Last Day ever written and it might be reasonable to suppose that the 'Sibylla' who testified with David is to be identified with the Erythraean who prophesied the end of the world. On the other hand, Celano may simply have meant the (unspecified) 'prophetess'. Nor is there any evidence that Giovanni Pisano recognized, or sought to portray, in his six sibyls on the Pistoia pulpit or the ten, of which five survive by studio assistants, on the Pisa pulpit, the variety of personality and of function in a theological sense which Michelangelo's five very distinct personages show on the Sistine Ceiling. This would be surprising in view of Giovanni's preoccupation with the appearance of individuals, unless the sibyls were in his day uncharacterized.

By the fifteenth century, the best-known sibyls were the Erythraean, the Cumaean, the Delphic, the Libyan, the Samian, the Hellespontine, the Persian, the Phrygian and the Tiburtine, who among them represented those parts of the Gentile world susceptible to Christian prophecy. The

Erythraean Sibyl in particular had been diplomatic enough to marry a son of Noah and pass into Jewish society, explaining meanwhile that she came from Babylon despite the claims of the Erythraeans. This, as Wind says,[12] showed 'a fine sense for the future union' of the Churches of Gentile and Jew. None of the niceties of nationality, nor those of temperament, are clear in Giovanni's carvings. Why then was he so concerned with sibyls? He remained alone in this preoccupation for well over a century and although he was more arbitrary in the numbering of them than was usual in a period when the precise number of virtues, liberal arts, deadly sins and so on was important, there is no doubt that the sibyls were important to the *summa* of the pulpits. In addition, there are the two female figures who join the prophets and pagan philosophers in foretelling the Incarnation of the Virgin on the Siena façade, and the unidentifiable figures of women, whom I believe to be sibyls, who crowned the pinnacles on the Pisa Baptistry.

One of the Siena sculptures is now known simply as 'a Sibyl' and it has been suggested that she represents the Erythraean[13] (her scroll reads *Et vocabitur Deus et Homo*); the other is known as 'Mary of Moses' or 'Miriam' and she is the most fiercely mantic figure in the whole canon of Giovanni's sculptures of women. Now the personal temperament of the sibyls in their later Christian tradition moved between the cool enlightenment shown by the Erythraean, through various degrees of learned intelligence such as that shown by the Persian in Michelangelo's fresco, to the mindless violence of god-struck inspiration of the Delphic and the ecstatic mystical clarity of the Libyan. Virgil's Cumaean prophetess is described in her frenzy whereas the Libyan Sibyl speaks of a transcendental light penetrating darkness. These degrees of mantic utterance were defined at their extremes by Plato as the one being below reason and the other above it, but this would seem not to have been known in the thirteenth century. In medieval terms their ways of foretelling were simply *visio*, the prophetic dream, and *somnium*, the enigmatic dream.

Given a period of doubt – and it is in times of emergency that oracles are consulted – the areas above and below reason are both exposed. In a sense such a distinction could be suggested as applying to the heated and lasting debates between the messianic Joachimites and the Thomist rationalists, but the distinction between the prophets and the sibyls was basically the distinction between those trained in the disciplines of Mosaic law and those in intuitive communication with God. Assuming that Giovanni had a choice in the matter of his imagery, the sibyl and his preoccupation with her could indicate the very disquiet his art so powerfully conveys in other particulars. If he had no such choice then whoever programmed his work at Siena, Pistoia and Pisa must have severally been concerned with sibyls, for it is remarkable that in so many different cities sibyls were required. Apart from his acknowledged statues of women called sibyls, at least one of the pinnacle figures on the Pisa Baptistry represents a woman listening intently among others who might, if they were complete, also be seen to be doing so. To what, if she is not a sibyl, does she listen, and what does the so-called 'Mary of Moses' at Siena do but utter what she has heard?

The imagery which was the source of Giovanni's sculpture was founded upon a shared Christian narrative in the process of rapid expansion; that expansion was required by the need to marry the humane to the numinous and by the need for worship by empathy. It was also a time when the ancient pagan world had been brought to act as witness to this marriage. So close indeed did this marriage between the ancient and the medieval worlds become that Gavin Douglas, the translator of the 'Thirteen' Aeneids, could 'interpret properly' the Cumaean Sibyl as a *figura* of the Blessed Virgin, calling her 'our Sibill, Christis moder deir'.[14] Such was the importance of Virgil to theologians and philosophers, quite apart from fabulists, that the messianic prophecies read into Book VI of the Aeneid and into the 4th Eclogue may well suggest an answer to the problem of Giovanni's vision of sibyls on the Pistoia and the Pisa pulpits. His sibyls resemble Madonnas not only as they are posed but in their drapery, which stems from French prototypes. There is no sign of mantic 'frenzy' in them, except for the 'Mary of Moses' on the Siena façade and one of the Pisa pinnacle figures. All of them listen, as the Madonna may commonly be seen to listen to the Annunciation. Are all of them *figurae* in which the ancient and the Christian worlds conjoin? It was no accident that it was Virgil who guided Dante on his journey through the Divine Comedy.

The Dominican *Legenda Aurea* had already had its effect and continued to do so but the *Meditationes Vitae Christi*, this time by a Franciscan, Giovanni de Caulibus (called the Pseudo-Bonaventura), was written whilst Giovanni was actually at work on the Pistoia pulpit. To the expanding legends of the life of the Virgin, the Pseudo-Bonaventura added the legend of the life of John the Baptist, part of which Giovanni incorporated in the narrative of his subsequent pulpit. This very process of expanding and therefore enriching apocryphal narrative must have created an atmosphere conducive to an acceptance of the living myth. It was a time of 'listening' and thence of 'speaking' not of new truths but of old ones suddenly enlarged. It is precisely this climate of thought which would give sibyls a special role, even if their individual identities had not yet clearly emerged, for not only do they speak expressly to the Gentiles but, unlike the more firmly established prophets, they are intuitive rather than learned.

To a largely illiterate laity, this fleshing out in Latin prose of the bare sacred bones of wise pagans, no less than those of dignitaries who had for long sat aloof upon the right hand of God, was a stage in the relationship between the Church and its communicants which was of great personal consequence to the individual. Once the Gospels and their attendant apocryphal stories were translated into the vernacular and spoken from the pulpit they were immediately significant, but in sculpture they could be *seen* to be believed and in painting were coming to be depicted with comparable credibility by Giotto and his followers as events at once ancient and contemporary. It is because the graven image has such a power to make the word flesh that iconoclasm can breed such fury. In Chapter I, verse 10, of the Apocalypse, St John cried: 'I was in the Spirit on the Lord's day, and heard behind me a great voice, as of a trumpet, saying, I am Alpha and Omega, the first and the last. . . .' The proliferation of words born from this affirmation is in the trumpet sound of that great voice and the primacy of medieval sculpture lay in giving visible and tangible form to such words.

If a question so obvious as to be absurd need be asked, namely: What is the Pistoia pulpit? the answer is a platform, for that is the origin of the word and it is a platform for *sound*. It is a structure intended to contain, embody and give vent to sound. It is the physical setting for the 'great voice as of a trumpet' transmuted but all-important. And sibyls and prophets are primarily vehicles of speech. Apart from his narrative reliefs and his Madonna groups, the greatest and certainly the most dynamic of all Giovanni Pisano's sculpture represents men and women in the act of speaking or listening to know of what they will speak. Upon the angles of the Pistoia pulpit a group of angels sound trumpets. The figures of the writers of the Canonical Epistles, dominated by St Paul, are seen and their letters were intended to be spoken aloud to the Corinthians, the Ephesians and other listening communities. Jeremiah utters his doom-laden prophecy, the symbols of the evangelists proclaim revelation and the mystical image of Christ embodies His Word.

Pl. 130

Pl. 142

Pls. 128, 129

Pl. 122

Pl. 127

The sixth angle figure represents a deacon whose presence emphasizes the purpose of the pulpit as a rostrum for the reading of the Gospels no less than for preaching. Thus in his capacity as reader the deacon's voice would also be heard.

The pulpit as a crystallization of meaningful sound and as such as one of the most perfectly conceived combinations of function and symbol in sculpture, reached its formal apex as sculpture in the Pistoia pulpit and its apex as a *summa* in the Pisa Cathedral pulpit, but all four of the pulpits by Nicola and Giovanni are without precedent and without comparable succession. This development in European sculpture coincided with a rising clamour of theological debate and a rapid expansion of Christian narrative. It occurred at a time when the Church was losing its spiritual authority and was doomed to go into 'Babylonian captivity' at Avignon.

Joachim da Fiore had foretold that the Church would cease to exist in 1260. It had survived. His Franciscan followers, seeing St Francis himself as the herald of the final phase of life on Earth, preached in church that the Church, weighed down with wealth and corruption, would fall. It did not. But in the dim light of the little church of S. Andrea today, the pulpit, one of the greatest complexes of relief sculpture in Christian art, stands in silence. I have never seen more than five people in its presence.

The Pulpit for the Church of S. Andrea, Pistoia

Full notes to the plates are on page 221

129

131

134

139

140

141

142

143

144

145

146

147

148

149

150

8 The Pisa Pulpit

Pls. 155–179 GIOVANNI'S FINAL and most elaborate pulpit was commissioned on behalf of the Pisa Cathedral authorities by the *Operaio* Burgundio di Tado in 1302. That this new commission should follow so hard upon the like one at Pistoia was probably the direct result of the latter's fame and the civic jealousy it induced in the Pisans. Medieval cities and city states competed in prestige with intense fervour and the Pisans would not readily have stood for so great a work in a neighbouring and rival city, especially since Pisa had given birth to its creator. Carrara marble was immediately quarried for a pulpit intended to be grander than that at Pistoia. By March 1302 it was cut and by November the slabs and blocks were transported from the quarries to Pisa. The work begun took nine years to complete. It began speedily but it did not go smoothly and from what documents survive there is no doubt that Giovanni and Burgundio di Tado were soon deeply at odds. In 1305 payments were registered for steel punches and drills, but the sparks struck between the sculptor and the *Operaio* were public enough to require a confirmation of Giovanni's contract, resulting from an enquiry by the Chapter. This specified that, should any conflict arise between the sculptor and Burgundio, a 'good and loyal man' satisfactory to Giovanni should replace the *Operaio*. As so often in such cases, the document provided for a contingency which had already arisen. Burgundio was relieved of direct responsibility and thereupon filed a suit against Giovanni or at least paid for the drafting of the action. The overt cause of the dispute seems to have been money, but if Burgundio withheld money owing to Giovanni which, by 1307, he had to pay up, it may be explained as readily by Giovanni's intemperate nature as by Burgundio's incompetent accounting. Either way, no further word on the matter has survived nor are there further documents on the continuing work on the pulpit. Burgundio remained *Operaio* until 1312 but was so pointedly excluded from Giovanni's long inscriptions on the pulpit that he was forced to put up his own plaque elsewhere in the Cathedral.[1]

Notes on page 206

The persons praised in Giovanni's upper inscription are one Nello di Falcone, whom he describes as controlling not only the work 'but also the rules upon which it was based', and Count Federigo da Montefeltro who at that time ruled in Pisa. What part Nello played in the quarrel, if any, is not known. Perhaps he either sided with Giovanni or avoided the issue. Nello, a member of an important 'new' Pisan family,[2] may indeed have been a churchman nominated by the Cathedral authorities, whom Giovanni was required to consult as to theological niceties in the narrative programme of the work. This being so, his talent for those inconographic acrostics and interlocking symbolical schemata must have been formidable indeed for the 'proper rules' evolved to relate the parts, and parts of parts, to each other and to the whole were more complicated in this pulpit than in any prototype. If Géza Jászai's[3] arguments are to be accepted, and I find them convincing, then the pulpit as it was originally designed and as it was orientated in relation to the choir and the nave of the cathedral, set forth a far more elaborate programme in terms of lateral, vertical and diagonal relationships than either Giovanni or Nicola had ever previously attempted.

As the pulpit stands today, in Bacci's reconstruction completed in 1926, it is an object of sculptural splendour but of theological confusion. Nevertheless it is incomparable, in terms of its time, except with Giovanni's other achievement at Pistoia, for none of his contemporaries, not even Arnolfo di Cambio, attempted anything so adventurous in relief carving, whilst their fellow pupil under Nicola, Fra Guglielmo, actually retrogressed from his master's example. His pulpit of 1270 in S. Giovanni Fuorcivitas at Pistoia is a simple rectangular structure carved in a convention from which Nicola himself broke away and from which Giovanni broke much farther. Among the younger generation, Tino da Camaino, Lorenzo Maitani and Andrea da Pontedera (known as Andrea Pisano) all reverted to the simpler tradition of the Gothic relief based on the tympanum, treating the dimension of depth with relatively little enterprise, despite their varied and very remarkable talents in other directions.

The size and elaboration of the Pisa Cathedral pulpit, in terms of labour, involved Giovanni in a greater degree of collaboration with his workshop than appears anywhere in the Pistoia pulpit. Furthermore, his supervision of these lesser talents seems in places to have been perfunctory. Once again the division of hands at work on the details of the sculpture has been much debated and remains unclear. Tino is believed to have participated, but this is far from certain, and among others the best-known of Giovanni's assistants were Giovanni di Simone, who was responsible for the construction of the Pisan Campo Santo, and Lupo di Francesco, who contributed largely to the little church of Sta Maria della Spina on the Arno. Both these structures have in the past been attributed to Giovanni himself, by Vasari and others, and both owe something at least to his inspiration. There were other craftsmen of less distinction at work on the pulpit and although Giovanni accepted full responsibility for the work, the inadequacy of parts of it, notably the Passion panel, the Elect at the Judgement, the St Michael, and, strangely enough, those of the sibyls which remain *in situ*, is clearly apparent.[4] These weaknesses doubtless played a part in bringing about the condemnation which Giovanni himself, in his inscription, says he received.

For the art historian, however sensitive and knowledgeable, however well equipped in applying such systems of individual identification as Morelli's, the relationship of a master to his studio assistant is far less readily established than even the most keen-eyed connoisseur or scholarly specialist may wish to believe. Even today, among living artists, when the degree of division of partial responsibility in the execution of a major work could be canvassed, it is not absolutely to be determined. Those of us who have worked with assistants know that the relationship can extend from the simplest manual labour, of greater or less competence, to an invaluably close and successful collaboration. How much more difficult is it fully to comprehend the nature of the relationship between master and pupil, artisan and labourer, in earlier times? The degree of identification with the master required of the executant in the fourteenth century in order that he should be able to sink himself into the eye and hand of that master and carry to completion, or near completion, a narrative sculpture as highly complex as Giovanni required has no parallel today. Certain levels, whether of incompetence or exceptional individuality, on the part of the assistant have made it possible for scholars to differentiate the hands in the execution of complex sculptural monuments with at least a moderate degree of confidence; but who can know how frustrated a master-sculptor may have been when he viewed the product of his request or command to tighten such and such a form or to articulate such and such a joint, only to find that in attempting it, his trusted workman had cut away too much? On the other hand, the master himself could have a bad day and have botched work which he would better have left to another. Art historians cannot take into account that such simple factors as a touch of rheumatics or eye-strain on a Monday may cause the hand to slip or the master's critical judgement to be blind. As sculptors, we are no longer used to medieval production methods. Furthermore, we have some technological aids which have been evolved since 1310 and although these may have done less than nothing to enhance our individual talents, they have affected our relationships with the craftsmen we employ. Those whose familiarity with such matters extends no further than their eyes, their photographic archives and their typewriters seldom have experience in this technical field and even if one does not have to be a hen to tell a bad egg, a cognisance of oviparous generation is useful on the farm. In marble carving of such technical difficulty and novelty as Giovanni's any substantial error in the workshop, even if it were possible to correct it to some degree, could not but grievously impair the work.

Nevertheless, the responsibility lay upon the master and in the most revealing and proudly defiant statement in the history of medieval art, Giovanni took that responsibility. In the inscription which now runs round the base of the pulpit he at once accepts and rebuffs his detractors in lines so remarkable that Vasari's abbreviation of them in his *Life of Giovanni* 'for fear of wearying the reader' is wholly surprising. The inscription reads:

CIRCUIT HIC AMNES   MUNDI PARTESQUE JOHANNES

PLURIMA TEMPTANDO   GRATIS DISCENDA, PARANDO

QUEQUE LABORE GRAVI   NUNC CLAMAT: NON BENE CAVI

DUM PLUS MONSTRAVI,   PLUS HOSTITA DAMNA PROBAVI.

CORDE SED IGNAVI   PENAM FERO MENTE SUAVI.

UT SIBI LIVOREM   TOLLAM MITIGEMQUE DOLOREM

ET DECUS IMPLOREM: VERSIBUS ADDE ROREM.

SE PROBAT INDIGNUM   REPROBANS DIADEMATE DIGNUM.

SIC HUNC QUEM REPROBAT   SE REPROBANDO PROBAT.

These lines, in careful, and not unskilful, Latin verse, are at once proud, bitter and resigned and if, in the fashion of the time, they are patient of more than one meaning,[5] they make themselves tragically clear: 'Giovanni has encircled here the rivers and the parts of the earth. Attempting much, freely learning and preparing all with great labour he now proclaims: I have not taken care enough, though I have achieved much I have been much condemned. Yet with an indifferent heart and a calm mind I bear the penalty. That I may avert hostility from this (the monument), mitigate my sorrow and seek glory (I say) join your tears to these verses. Let him who reproves (this work) prove himself, unworthy one, worthy of the crown. Thus he who is reproved proves himself and proves (also) the worth of the reprover.'

It is a world apart from the tenor of the inscription which runs below the upper half of this same 'much condemned' pulpit. Immediately beneath the narrative panels run the words:

LAUDO DEUM VERUM   PER QUEM SUNT OPTIMA RERUM

QUI DEDIT HAS PURAS   HOMINEM FORMARE FIGURAS.

HOC OPUS HIC ANNIS   DOMINI SCULPSERE JOHANNIS

ARTE MANUS SOLE   QUONDAM NATIQUE NICHOLE

CURSUS UNDENIS   TERCENTUM MILLEQUE PLENIS

JAM DOMINANTE PISIS   CONCORDIBUS ATQUE DIVISIS

COMITE TUNC DICO   MONTISFELTRO FREDERICO

HIC ASSISTENTE   NELLO FALCONIS, HABENTE

HOC OPUS IN CURA   NEC NON OPERE QUOQUE IURA.

EST PISIS NATUS   UT JOHANNES ISTE DOTATUS

ARTIS SCULPTURE   PRE CUNCTIS ORDINE PURE

SCULPENS IN PETRA   LIGNO AURO SPLENDIDA, TETRA

SCULPERE NESCISSET   VEL TURPIA SI VOLUISSET.

PLURES SCULPTORES: REMANENT SIBI LAUDIS HONORES.

CLARAS SCULPTURAS   FECIT VARIASQUE FIGURAS.

QUISQUIS MIRARIS   TUNC RECTO JURE PROBARIS.

CRISTE MISERERE   CUI TALIA DONA FUERE.   AMEN

The distinction of tone between these two inscriptions on the same monument is extraordinary: 'I praise the true God, the creator of all excellent things who has permitted a man to form figures with such purity. In the year of our Lord thirteen hundred and eleven, the hands of Giovanni son of the late Nicola, by their own art alone, carved this work while there ruled the Pisans Count Federigo Montefeltro, and at his side Nello di Falcone who, working together and yet separately, has exercised control not only of the work but also of the rules on which it is based. He is a Pisan by birth, like that Giovanni who is endowed above all others with command of the pure art of sculpture, sculpting in stone, wood and gold, splendid things. He could not carve base ones even if he wished. There are many sculptors but to him only remain the praises and honour. He has made noble sculpture and varied figures. Let those who marvel at them give him their rightful approval. Christ have mercy on him to whom such gifts are given. Amen.'

How could this man, rightly conscious of his genius, who at Pistoia had haughtily described himself as possessed of greater gifts than his father, first ask the public to wonder at his achievements and then require them, however rhetorically, to weep as they cast their eyes downward a matter of two and a half metres? What intolerable burden of anxiety, fatigue or plain circumstantial frustration would cause a man 'endowed above all others with the pure art of sculpture' and so clearly unendowed with modesty, to make such a confession of failure even as he metaphorically shakes his fist in the face of the unworthy who would dare to seek to prove themselves worthy of the crown.

Doubtless there are grave flaws in the execution of details of the pulpit and clearly Giovanni's boast that none but his hands carved the marble was a rhetorical one. It must also be remembered that today the pulpit is so placed and so orientated in the Cathedral as to be deprived of both the cohesion and the meaning by which Giovanni and Nello must have set their greatest store.[6] Even given certain flaws in execution, it contained, on the credit side, not only an unparalleled intellectual scheme but innovations in the use of perspective in the treatment of the scale of foreground and background figures and blazing bursts of dramatic power which strike home with the sharp shock of revelation. Yet in its total impact it seems today to be strange, disturbing and uneasy, largely because our priorities in what we require of such a work are so remote from those of the first decade of the fourteenth century.

John White, in his admirable chapter on the pulpit,[7] proposes the wholly sensible explanation that 'it must have taxed the artist's powers of invention to embark upon a second pulpit almost as soon as his first was finished' and that 'the need to create more than a second version of the Pistoia Pulpit must have been pressing. On the structural side,' he continues, 'the challenge was triumphantly met by exploiting the rich vein of classicism always present in his art.' He ascribes the failure to achieve a successful new synthesis to 'the lack of a sufficient interval to refresh his mind and consolidate new ground' before embarking on the larger, more ambitious and more challenging pulpit at Pisa. This is contestable only in certain particulars but they are important. The comparative failure of the work as a whole lies in a conceptual complexity so dense that perhaps it was self-defeating even in its own day, for even if it stood now as whole and as correctly assembled as upon the day it was completed it would reveal *far more information* than the spectator could absorb in the absence of a more absolute formal perfection of detail. St Gregory's teaching that such works of art were the 'books' of the illiterate laity held only at a time when acceptance of the content of the books was so little in question that their form was of minor concern, but as the plastic arts increased in visual sophistication, at the dawn of the Renaissance, the spectator came to require his attention held not only by the meaning of the subject but by the form of it and so the balance of form and content became crucial. Giovanni's 'fault' confessed in his inscription surely lay in giving to the learned an overplus of the abstruse information they required at the expense of their aesthetic needs. So complex was the structure that St Gregory's illiterate laity would hardly have been more readily able to 'read' the pulpit than they would the 'book' and doubtless it was not their views in the matter that were canvassed. It is not the programme of the Sistine Chapel ceiling which holds the twentieth-century spectator spellbound, although he must be aware of an enormous intellectual structure underlying the visual achievement; it is a cohesion of mind and pictorial performance so great that the iconography may be taken as read because no disbelief requires to be suspended nor any doctrine transmitted for the work to convince. On the other hand, it is the vast complex of interlocked ideas whose very existence, whether or not even a fraction of them is comprehended, which inspires overwhelming awe when realized with Michelangelo's formal genius.

If Giovanni had brought to the Pisa pulpit the full flooding power of which he had proved himself capable, the very complexity of the edifice would have contributed to and not diminished its success. *Non bene cavi* was rightly inscribed upon the monument and we may indeed join our tears to his verses however unworthy we may be of the crown. This unhappy slackening of total control of detail, added to the personal difficulties, the rivalries, the malice, the financial disputes and other unknown sources of discontent, the nature of which are long lost through the passage of time, may have been enough to destroy the balance and undermine the tenacity of purpose Giovanni needed to follow the faultless work at Pistoia with an ever greater triumph at Pisa.

There is, however, another possibility which I believe should not be discounted. When Giovanni revealed himself in the words *Non bene cavi* he came near, given the difference between a medieval public inscription and a private Renaissance sonnet, to revealing the area of self-doubt which sometimes flaws and yet confirms the very greatest art and especially the greatest dramatic and narrative art. It is the Promethean vulture finding another liver upon which to feed. It is Michelangelo's tragic, paradoxical and insupportable liberty to fail in later life which is prefigured in Giovanni's last pulpit, when the vision cannot be contained within the mould no matter what preparation of great labour has gone into the making of it, when the heart despairs not from the condemnation of hostile critics but from the inescapable self-inflicted malady of self-doubt. That Giovanni protests too much does not suggest to me that he cared about the attacks and envious malice, if such it was, of Burgundio di Tado or anyone else, but that – no longer believing in himself for spiritual or personal reasons we can never know – he dropped his eyes from the summit as it came within his reach.

The forms of the lions which support two of the columns of the Pisa Cathedral pulpit are taken *Fig. o* from a Roman sarcophagus now in the Campo Santo; the lions and lioness of Nicola may well have come from a similar source. Nicola's lions in the Pisa Baptistry have their prey alive and comfortable *Pl. 154* between their paws, the lioness nurses her cubs. They are not menacing creatures. At Pistoia, Giovan- *Cat. 266* ni's lioness also nurses her cubs and does no more harm to the frightened rabbit at her feet than does Nicola's although the lion has seized its prey in its jaws. But the two lions which support Giovanni's *Pls. 177, 178* final pulpit are agape with anguished rage. When Moore saw them he grasped the jaws of one in his hands and cried that they were roaring out 'the blackness of hell or something'. And the disembowel- led horse, its eye glazing in death, whose head one lion presses down, no less than the twisted wreckage of the deer the other grapples, are images more terrible than any damned at the Judgement on any pulpit. The bones of victor and vanquished jut like axe-blades beneath their stone skins. They are not the conventional guardians of Romanesque doorways but the forms of killer and slain released by action from the stone into the perpetual action of guarding the Church from the menace of unseen external forces, and showing the overthrow of Anti-Christ.

As Dante goes upwards through Purgatory he comes upon a curving terrace above a precipice, and gazing upon this circling bank he sees:

> *esser di marmo candido e adorno*
> *d'intagli sì che non pur Policreto*
> *ma la natura lì avrebbe scorno*

that it is carved in relief in pure white marble with such skill that not only Polycletus but Nature herself were put to shame. He stands rejoicing in these carved images of humilities, finding them precious for their craftsman's sake, and he recognizes that he is contemplating a *visible speech* new to him because no such sculptures exist in the ordinary world, but that they were made by one who had never beheld a new thing.

> *Colui che mai non vide cosa nuova*
> *produsse esto visibile parlare,*
> *Novello a noi perchè qui non su trova.*
> *Mentr'io mi dilettava di guardare*
> *le imagini di tante umilitadi*
> *e per lo fabbro loro a veder care;*

Virgil causes him to look to the left and there he discerns a group of people, each one bent under a great burden of stone. They are the Proud. Then Virgil tells him to be comforted and not to heed the pain of those proud in this special way, for they are worms born to form the angelic butterfly that flies to judgement without defence.

How apt these passages are to Giovanni in all particulars, and although it was not the pulpits but Trajan's column that the poet may have had in mind, how apt these words are even in date, for the *Purgatorio* was written in about 1312, a year after the completion of the Pisa Cathedral pulpit, and the quotations are from Canto X.

Full notes to the plates are on page 223

157

158

159

160

161

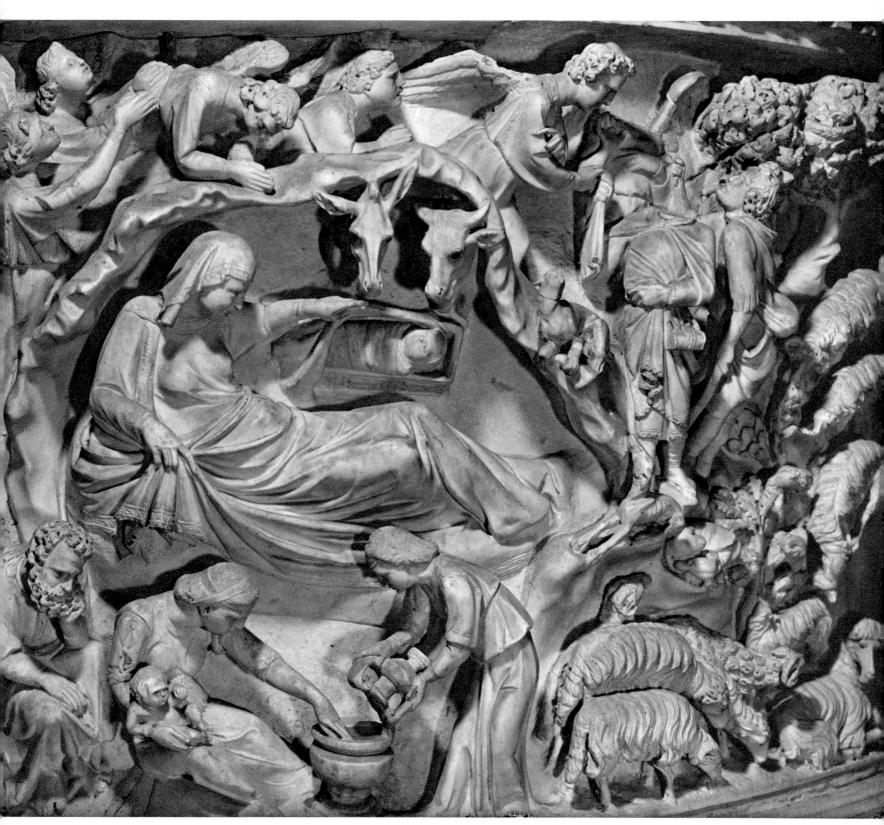

163

169

170

171

172

176

9 *The Last Sculptures*

THE PISA CATHEDRAL PULPIT, whatever caused Giovanni to apportion so much of the labour to his workshop, is charged with the final flood of that furious energy which represents the Dionysiac drive in him. Even where a whole area of carving lies slack, it is possible to mark where the master took up his chisel to galvanize a group into vital action; the lower line of figures in the otherwise un-inspired panel of the Elect rising at the Judgement is a case in point. But the daemon that had possessed him since the days when, for the last time, he worked with his father on the colossi for the Baptistry Façade and which charged even these undemonstrative giants with a titanic, if latent energy, left him forever when he stood self-condemned before his last pulpit in 1311. For the remainder of his life his work, or what remains to us of his last sculptures, is classically calm. The Apollonian sense of order which had invariably given tranquillity to his Madonna groups now reigned undisturbed. Whether a personal crisis had passed, what rage had subsided in him, we cannot know, but his classicism is no longer Hellenistic. To find a comparison is to go back beyond the age of Pericles.

Pl. 165

If he was born in 1250, he was now a man of sixty-one. Of his personal life we still know practically nothing save that he was wealthy enough to have made a substantial loan to some woolworkers, but this does not take us further than the scant information which remains to us of his earlier business dealings. A document informs us that in 1299 a deed had been drawn up in Pisa wherein Giovanni agreed to purchase a house near the Cathedral of Siena from a lady called Donna Pardo, the proceeds of the sale to be used to set up her two sons as marble-workers, that being their father's trade. However tempting it may be to read any motive other than a commercial one into this interesting transaction, there is no evidence to support it. One can only speculate idly on what Donna Pardo, the single woman ever mentioned in direct connection with Giovanni, may have been to him and on the identity of the father of the future marble-workers. All we have is the contract. As to his activities in Siena after 1299 there is no mention of him in connection with the Cathedral. Camaino di Crescentino, the father of Giovanni's follower, Tino, eventually attained the title of *capomaestro* there.

All that otherwise remains touching upon his private life is a document dated 9th March 1314 giving judgement on an appeal against a tax demand. The Constable of the Siena Commune had attempted to claim tax on both Giovanni's houses, the one he had bought from Donna Pardo and another acquired at the same time, together with land, in the Pian de Vignolo. Giovanni appealed to the *Consiglio*, citing his long-established immunity from taxation which had not been repealed, and still appears on the record in 1309 and 1310. The Council voted on the matter and resolved in Giovanni's favour, with one hundred and eighty-seven voting in his favour and seventeen against him. Whether or not seventeen consequential citizens still believed, after seventeen years, that Giovanni had been culpable in the scandal of the marble yard, a very large majority obviously believed either that the fault had lain elsewhere or that it were best forgotten. His immunity continued through the remainder of his life.

At some point, not exactly dated, during his work on the final pulpit at Pisa, Giovanni received and fulfilled for Enrico Scrovegni of Padua an order for a marble Madonna and Child with attendant angels. This was to be placed in what has come to be called the 'Arena Chapel', in Scrovegni's native city, a building he caused to be erected in expiation of the sins of his father, whose fortune, gained from usury, moved Dante to set him firmly in the seventh circle of Hell. The continuing fame of the 'Arena Chapel' derives of course from the great fresco-cycle Giotto painted for it, and although the exact dates are not securely established, the frescoes were painted between 1304 and 1313. Giovanni's sculptures, all too often overlooked among the splendours of Giotto's overwhelming achievement, were carved in Pisa during the period in which Giotto was working at Padua, but there is no evidence that Giovanni actually went to Padua, nor is it absolutely certain that Giotto and Giovanni ever met, although Vasari maintains that they did.[1] There is, however, no doubt that the Madonna carved for Scrovegni by Giovanni was an indication of his widely established fame. Scrovegni spared no expense, and in employing Giotto and Giovanni upon his pious undertaking he was certainly aware that he had acquired the services of masters of the first rank.

The Madonna bears a marked resemblance to the earlier carving for the tympanum of the Pisa Baptistry door, for which reason it may also have been designed for a lintel rather than for the altar upon which it now stands. Fortunately, it must long ago have reached its present destination, for unlike the earlier sculpture it has obviously never been subject to the weathering which has destroyed most of the surface of the Pisa tympanum figure. The Padua Madonna is as relaxed as her Pisan counterpart is tense and her drapery falls in fluid folds where those of the earlier figure are pulled strongly and laterally across the form. Freed from stress, the Padua Madonna carries the Child lower

Pl. 121
Cat. 274–276

Notes on page 206

Pls. 119, 120

on the hip and He returns her grave glance with a look of enquiry as if He sought to learn from her the gravity of all that would follow. The two angels which flank the Madonna are usually ascribed to the master's workshop. If they are not from his hand, they are of high enough quality to have been carved under his close supervision. The Madonna herself bears the inscription: '*Deo Gratias* † *Opus Johannis Magistri Nicoli de Pisis.*'

Cat. 274, 276

Three more major works by Giovanni remain to us after the completion of the Pisa pulpit. Of these, two are linked in circumstances of tragic irony, for one was made to honour the Emperor Henry VII and completed between his coronation on 29 July 1312 and his death from fever outside Siena 13 months later on 29 August 1313, whilst the other was the tomb of the Emperor's wife Margaret of Luxembourg, who had predeceased his coronation by only a few months, dying of the plague at Genoa in December 1311. Both these monumental works exist today in fragments. The 'Madonna di Arrigo' was undertaken at the direction of the same Burgundio di Tado with whom Giovanni had quarrelled seven years earlier. Once again his appointment as *Operaio* must have weighed heavily on him as he faced the unavoidable task of directing Giovanni, if the latter permitted any such direction. At all events, the relationship did not last, for Burgundio was gone by 1313, but the inscription beneath the Madonna indicates that matters had been at least formally reconciled between them.

Pl. 153

The 'Madonna di Arrigo' originally consisted of a Madonna and Child, of which only a substantial but shattered fragment remains; the figure of the Emperor, which is now lost; and the symbolic figure representing the city of Pisa, whose head was rediscovered in 1936 among the fragments in that graveyard of graveyards, the storehouse of the Campo Santo. This, joined to the surviving trunk of the figure, shows Pisa kneeling in homage to the Madonna. Originally the Emperor also knelt to the Madonna and the group stood over the lintel of the door of St Ranieri at the East Front of the nave of Pisa Cathedral opposite the Campanile, where it bore the inscription: '*Ave Maria Gratia Plena Dominus Tecum Nobilis Arte Manus Sculpsit Johannes Pisanus Sculpsit sub Burgundio Tadi Benigno*' on the now missing base of the Madonna.[2] The 'Pisa' bore the inscription: '*Virginis Ancilla sub Pisa quieta sub illa*' and the statue of the Emperor was subscribed: '*Imperat Henricus qui Christo Fertur Amicus.*' The benign Burgundio whose name had been omitted from the Pisa pulpit inscription and who had been forced to put up his own plaque in the Cathedral, claiming his share of honour, achieved it at least for several centuries below the 'Madonna di Arrigo'. Not however for longer; the group was taken down during the seventeenth century and the Madonna placed in the church of S. Martino in Kinsica where it was struck by lightning in 1810. The other figures were stored in a shed. Between 1821 and 1829 the shattered Madonna was re-erected in the Campo Santo, where in 1930 it was recognized as the work of Giovanni.[3] Thus the short-lived Emperor was honoured by a sculpture which suffered an even worse fate than the other external sculptures by Giovanni which are today so worn by the elements. The tomb of the Countess who did not even live to see her husband

Cat. 278

crowned was already in course of work and a payment of 81 gold florins for it had been made in the name of the Emperor, when he too died. Giovanni left for Genoa on 29 August 1312 and received the 81 gold florins there from the archdeacon of the church, but the tomb, which was carved from Carrara marble, was almost certainly transported from Pisa in sections and erected in S. Francesco di Casteletto in Genoa, where it remained until it too was destroyed, together with the church in which it stood, in 1798. Until 1960 only the upper half of the figure of Margaret herself, attended by two headless angels, was known to have survived the destruction of the tomb. These fragments alone are remarkable enough, for not only are they among the most moving in all his work but they have no precedent in Italian sculpture. The subtle swing of the attendant angels as they raise the apparently almost weightless figure of Margaret from the tomb is a slow and very delicate version of Giovanni's famous 'dramatic twist'. And as an added touch which would have been invisible but which is radical, the drapery of Margaret's headdress is drilled clear through down both sides of her face in order that light could reach her cheeks.

Pls. 180–183

Just as the head of 'Pisa' was rediscovered in 1930, so in 1960 and 1962 two further parts of the lost tomb of Margaret came to light in Genoa. Both found by Dr Caterina Marcenaro,[4] the sculptures are those of a Madonna and the figure of Justice. The latter is complete, and considering the fate of the tomb itself, relatively undamaged. She is small and in such just proportion to the figure of Margaret and to the now headless and more seriously damaged Madonna, that allowing for perspective in the siting of the figures on the monument, the hypothesis that all were parts of a single structure cannot be doubted. The 'Justice', in comparison to her counterpart below the Pisa pulpit, is heavily built and stately. A woman in middle age as opposed to elderly, the Genoa figure wears an expression of patient concern and even perplexity, whereas at Pisa she is stern and pitiless. She is as one whose duty it is to judge but who has not reached a final judgement and she carries her scales not in her hand but upon her breast, wearing them like a plastron as if, metaphorically, they serve as the source of mercy or at least of charity.

Cat. 278

Pls. 184–186

Pl. 173

The change of psychological emphasis is striking. All that was frenetic and tense in the Pisa pulpit and inflexible in the countenance of the Pisa 'Justice' is calmed. All that was sinewy and urgent has become ample and weighty and so too with the Madonna who, for all that she has lost everything that could be broken from her and stands as stripped as her classical forerunners from the Parthenon pediment, has about her an organic wholeness which raises her to the topmost height of classical medieval sculpture.

Pls. 187, 188

Some idea, albeit in an uninspired form, of what the Madonna and the four Virtues, of which the 'Justice' was one, must originally have looked like, remains in Genoa, in the Church of the Maddalena, where a group of marbles by a modest artisan at work in the 1350's show a marked similarity to the two carvings by Giovanni.

The fragments of the monument to Margaret of Luxembourg are the only surviving evidence of Giovanni's activity as a tomb sculptor, an activity, if Vasari is to be believed, which formed a substantial part of his life's work. His father, his fellow pupil under Nicola, Arnolfo, and his best-known follower, Tino, have all left funerary sculpture of high quality, and indeed Tino specialized in this branch of his art. Upon Nicola's design for the Arca of St Dominic at Bologna, Arnolfo worked with Lapo and Fra Guglielmo among others, and emerged as immeasurably their superior. He found his own style in working upon that monument and, removed to Rome at the completion of Nicola's Siena pulpit, his first independent commission was the Annibaldi monument. This was followed by other sepulchral monuments, notably that of Pope Adrian V and that of Cardinal de Braye, which survives at Orvieto.

No sculptors of comparable stature could be more antithetical than Giovanni and Arnolfo; their arts grew in wholly different directions from the stem of Nicola. Tino, on the other hand, who is presumed to have been trained in Giovanni's workshop, was thirty years younger than his master and lived for thirty years after Arnolfo's death. In 1315 he became *capomaestro* of Pisa Cathedral and in the same year received the commission to carve the funeral monument for the ill-fated Emperor Henry VII, parts of which may still be seen in the Campo Santo. In Florence, and thereafter in Naples, he spent most of his life on the carving of tombs. Much argument has been generated over the part Tino played in carving, under Giovanni, the 'Madonna di Arrigo', and various small Madonnas which are now regarded as early works by Tino have, in the past, been attributed to Giovanni. If therefore Giovanni's tomb for Margaret of Luxembourg was influential, Tino doubtless learned from it.

The image of Margaret being raised from her tomb at Genoa has no precedent, but it is possible that the 'Madonna di Arrigo' has. It bears a marked resemblance in pose to the small Madonna carved in wood in the first decade of the *trecento* and now at Orvieto. This woodcarving, as I remarked on p. 87, has been attributed by Carli to Giovanni's rival at Siena, the mysterious Ramo di Paganello.

Pl. 122
Fig. v

In groping among the fragile and fugitive strands of inference which cloak the life, as opposed to the art, of Giovanni Pisano, one finds so many broken in the course of time that nothing save intuition and insight are left to bring the man into any sort of focus. Is the personal crisis which he may have suffered after the completion of the Pistoia pulpit substantiated by the inscription on the Pisa pulpit? Is the lackadaisical fashion in which he appears to have delegated major parts of that work to the secondary talents of his workshop symptomatic of a profound fatigue weighing upon the spirit? And was Tino a part of that workshop? If so, why does his personality fail to emerge there?

I have tried to suggest that some personal response to the theological conflicts of the time affected Giovanni and it is of course possible that, as his pupil Tino[5] came to be in 1315–16, he too was involved at some time in that fratricidal opposition of factions that was the bane of the time.

There is no evidence for either of these conjectures, and yet, to consider his life-span from the failure of the great project at Siena through the triumph at Pistoia to the condemnation of his pulpit at Pisa, and thence to see him rise phoenix-like from the ashes to the majestic and tranquil achievements of his final years, is to know as much and more about Giovanni than one can know about his contemporaries or predecessors among the sculptors of the final phase of the Middle Ages.

He was a proud and difficult man, large in proper conceit, quick to anger. Perhaps he was too ready to lay aside his tools in anger or despair, leaving work upon which he had spent himself 'attempting much and preparing all with great labour', but then the way in which medieval masters allocated work to their assistants and seemingly accepted the results, is not readily comprehensible to us. Since the rise of the artist as demigod, to which we have become accustomed once Michelangelo had come to be called 'Il Divino', we have long ceased to regard sculptures as *tanti umilitadi* and come to concentrate our esteem upon the converse.

Giovanni lived at a time when our notion of the artist as an individual to be valued uniquely for the unique product of his own hands had barely emerged. It is in no small measure due to him that it did emerge, for he stands out from his time as the first craftsman quite so forcefully to demand attention in this rôle. His passion joined to his energy gave his sculpture a force greater than any, not only in his time but until Michelangelo came to rival him, and the Promethean power he shared with Michelangelo earned for him a share in the Promethean nemesis. When Michelangelo failed to complete individual sculptures because his vision outran even his prodigious power to give it tangible form, his time and his enormous celebrity usually, but not invariably, earned him the right to leave such works unfinished. This could not have happened two centuries earlier. When Giovanni despaired of completion it would not have occurred to his contemporaries to leave the matter there. It was not an attitude which reflected humility in the sculptor, nor a proper attitude to his function, nor would it have been considered acceptable practice. Convention can only be successfully flouted when the time is ripe.

If, as it sometimes seems, the fates play a rôle above and apart from the affairs of men, then the irony with which the elements have been manipulated by these unseen forces to grind and weather away, to strike with lightning and shatter in conflict and conflagration the marbles Giovanni carved, melt down his work in gold and break or burn his work in ivory, if they have treated his sin of pride as it deserved, it is we who are the losers. And yet the irony circles inexhaustibly for we belong to an age when the fragment can often evoke more magic for us than unblemished perfection. Margaret of Luxembourg as she is raised marvelling from the grave, her broken face alight with wonder, by angels who, as they sway to bear her upwards, perform their wondrous and final action headless, is today isolated from all her formal and unknowable marble context. She wakes as if released at last from some incorporeal shell, her close-wrapped cerements the placenta of her new birth. Then too the juggling fates have, during the last forty years, been gathering and restoring to us the fragments of Giovanni's last major works. Justice has returned bearing a sword and a scroll in which are cut the words '*Dilecisti justitiam odisti iniquitatem*'. She carries, too, an earthbound weight of drapery, as heavy as Margaret's slender form is light. The Madonna from the tomb is also newly found, just as the Madonna of the Emperor Henry and her attendant Pisa were rediscovered a generation ago. The piecing together of fragments is not necessarily at an end.

In September 1968, when this text had been completed in draft, a further fragment of

Pl. 189   Margaret's tomb was published. It is the head of the figure of Temperance, which has been identified by Dr Max Seidel,[6] and it is the single known work by Giovanni Pisano still in private hands, for it was acquired by a Swiss collector in 1942. Like the recently recovered figure of Justice and the still

Pls. 184–186   missing Fortitude and Prudence, the Temperance was part of a group which stood below the now

Pls. 187, 188   mutilated figure of the Madonna, also newly recovered. The anonymous artisan whose copies of Giovanni's figures for the tomb are preserved in S. Maria Maddalena in Genoa showed Temperance with a finger laid to her lips in a silencing gesture which derives from the third chapter of the Epistle to St James, where it is referred to as *mansuetudo*, that virtue which bridles men's tongues, preventing them from offending by their words. Aquinas' system of virtues brings this self-assumed bridle under Temperance, and where Giotto in the Arena Chapel shows the Virtue actually wearing a bridle, the finger was all Giovanni needed.[7] The mark where the silencing finger lay is still discernible upon the Virtue's lips.

Pl. 123   One small marble carving, *La Madonna della Cintola*, makes up the sum of the sculpture by Giovanni Pisano at present known. She is wholly undamaged and what minor blemishes she wears are not the result of destruction but of addition, for piety has added to her brow a tawdry gilt and jewelled crown and to her Child a gilt wire halo. Although this little sculpture is undocumented, the correctness of its attribution has never been questioned. The probable date may be gauged by a circumstance involving loss and return strangely in parallel to the loss and gradual recovery of the fragments of the monuments to the Emperor Henry and his wife. In 1312, the Girdle of the Virgin, which had lain in the Cathedral at Prato since 1100, was stolen and then ransomed. It is probable that in celebration of this recovery, Giovanni received the commission to carve this, perhaps his last Madonna,[8] for the altar of the Chapel of the Holy Girdle, where she stands today whispering to her Child in that 'visible speech, new to us for here it is not found'. She is the gayest of his Madonnas. In her, and in her Son, the Passion preordained is not prefigured, and if the presumed date of the carving is accurate, she shares with the Madonna for the tomb of Margaret, Giovanni's last thoughts on the subject. If this is so, they are very different thoughts, for the Genoa Madonna is all *gravitas*.

To the end of his life Giovanni remained a citizen of Siena and at the end of his life he went back to Siena. He had selected his place of burial by the left flank of the Cathedral and in the plain silver-grey wall near the door of the Vescovato may still be seen a stone incised with an abbreviation of the legend: *Hic est Sepulcrum Magistri Johannis quondam Magistri Nicole et ejus eredibus.*

No one knows when he died. By inference the obliteration of that statute which granted him tax immunity is taken to mark the fact that he was no longer living in 1319.

There is nothing remarkable about the fact that in the documents of 1310 and 1314 which relate to this challenged privilege, Giovanni is never referred to as anything but *magister* or *magister lapidorum;* after all, he had long ceased to work for the Siena Cathedral authorities. On the other hand, who in that age, in all of Europe, stood better entitled by virtue of his genius to the title *caput magistrorum?*

182

183

184

185

187

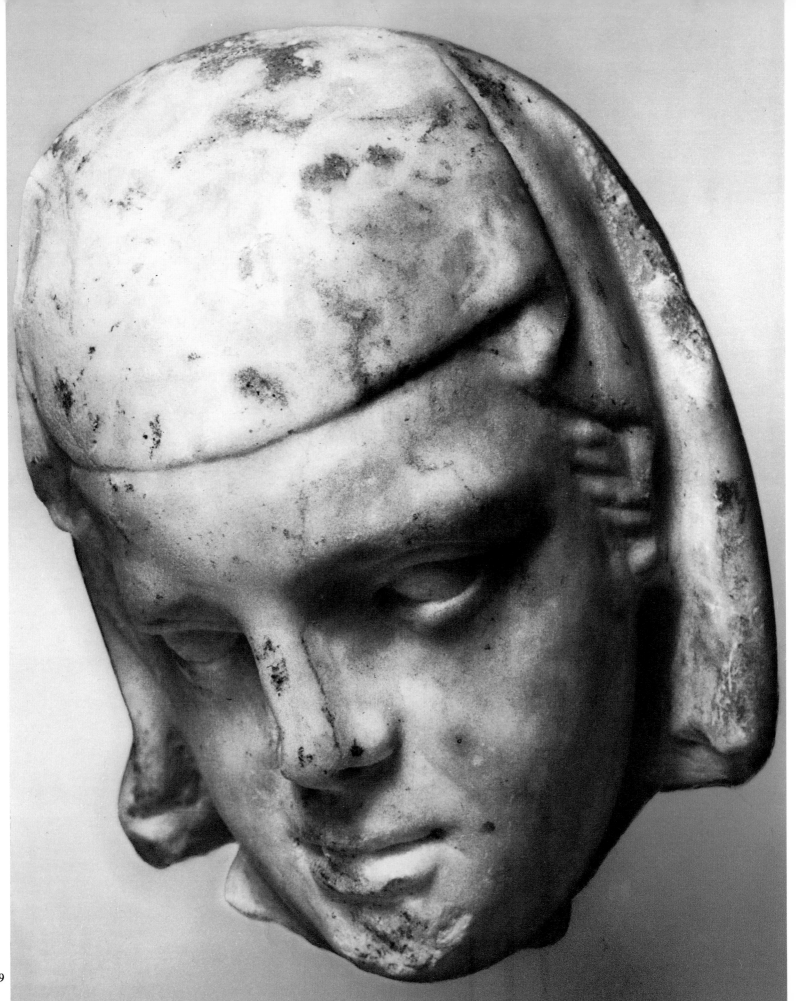

189

PREFACE

1 John Pope-Hennessy, *Italian Gothic Sculpture* (London, Phaidon, 1955). John White, *Art and Architecture in Italy, 1250–1400* in the Penguin History of Art (Harmondsworth, 1966).

2 G. H. and E. R. Crichton, *Nicola Pisano and the Revival of Sculpture in Italy* (Cambridge, 1938). G. Swarzenski, *Nicola Pisano* (Frankfurt, 1926). G. N. Fasola, *Nicola Pisano* (Rome, 1941).

3 E. Carli, *Il Pulpito di Siena* (Bergamo, 1943).

4 G. N. Fasola, *La Fontana di Perugia* (Rome, 1951).

5 Three important fragments of this tomb have been identified since 1960, but only two actually came upon the market.

6 Two Sibyls from this pulpit were in Berlin but were destroyed by fire in 1945.

7 Robert Dan Wallace, *L'Influence de la France gothique sur deux précurseurs de la Renaissance Italienne: Nicola et Giovanni Pisano* (Geneva, 1953).

1 THE GOTHIC FRAME

1 G. G. Coulton, *The Fall of Medieval Art*, Part II (New York, Harper Bros., 1958), pp. 413–16, maintained that this architectural afforestation was the direct result of thicker and higher forests in the north of Europe than in the south. He reinforced his argument by pointing out that only one Gothic church was built in Rome and that churches in Italy and southern France 'never ran so high' as those in the north. He sums up with the 'literal truth' that 'the nearer to Rome the farther from Gothic'. The density of the forests surrounding medieval Pisa provided one of the city's major trades but perhaps the trees there were less tall than those north of the Alps.

2 John Larner, 'The Artists and the Intellectuals in 14th century Italy', in *History*, LIV, No. 180 (1969), p. 14.

3 Erwin Panofsky, *Gothic Architecture and Scholasticism* (New York, Meridian Books, 1957).

4 The first clear sign of this novel thought appears in the *Decameron* when Boccaccio refers to Giotto as 'bringing to life the art that for many centuries had been buried beneath the errors of those who in painting sought to give pleasure to the eyes of the ignorant rather than delight to the minds of the wise'.

5 This tendency for sculpture to move out from its niche is earlier if less dramatically illustrated by the figures carved by the 'Master of Joseph' for Reims Cathedral.

6 Pope-Hennessy, *op. cit.*, p. 3.

2 NICOLA PISANO AND THE CLIMATE OF HIS TIME

1 That Nicola as a master sculptor could have been a learned man is not impossible. His French contemporary, the architect Pierre de Montereau, who died in 1267, is described on his tomb as 'Doctor Lathomorum'.

2 Dante, *Epistola X*.

3 Walafried Strabo of Fulda identified John with Air, Matthew with Earth, Luke with Fire and Mark with Water.

4 J. G. Davies, *The Architectural Setting of Baptism* (London, Barrie & Rockliffe, 1962).

5 The subjection of the secular clergy was complete well before Clement IV decreed the disposal of all vacant bishoprics at the court of Rome in 1266.

6 John Moorman, *The History of the Franciscan Order* (Oxford, 1968) also E. Gilson, *The Philosophy of St Bonaventure* (London, Sheed & Ward, 1938).

7 The history of the decline of medieval Pisa, together with details of her economy, government and communications system, is admirably outlined in D. Herlihy, *Pisa in the Early Renaissance* (Yale, 1958). Among other relevant details Herlihy remarks that in the early thirteenth century iron workers and building workers constituted Pisa's largest professional community, that her trade in fabricated iron (tools, armour etc.) declined towards the end of the century and that her

colonies in the Middle East had so shrunk as to be consolidated at Acre until that city fell to the Saracens in 1291. Thereafter the Pisans retreated to Cyprus. Herlihy also suggests that malaria played a part in Pisa's collapse.

8 Leslie Aitchison, *A History of Metals* (London, Macdonald & Evans, 1960), p. 302.

9 C. Bluemel, *Greek Sculptors at Work* (London, Phaidon, 1955), pp. 80–3.

10 Harald Keller, *Giovanni Pisano* (Vienna, 1942).

11 Bluemel, *op. cit.*, also refers to and reproduces two unfinished marbles of the early fourteenth century in the museum at Orvieto, which were produced in the same fashion as the unfinished Pisan relief.

12 Arnolfo's figures for the façade of Florence Cathedral were removed from it well before a nineteenth-century industrial atmosphere could attack them.

13 Traces of Giovanni's cunning employment of vitreous paste to add to the impression of depth behind the figures in relief on his Pistoia pulpit may still be discerned there, especially on the panel of the Nativity.

14 The much repainted marble relief figures on the lunettes of the Parma Baptistry by Benedetto Antelami, carved at the opening of the thirteenth century, show clearly the extent to which polychrome sculpture could be married to wall painting. This relationship too was prefigured by the archaic Greeks.

3 Giovanni, Son of Nicola: Siena and Perugia

1 The contract and specifications are published in full by E. Carli in *Il Pulpito di Siena* (Bergamo, 1943), pp. 45–8.

2 K. G. Frey, *Vasari. Le Vite* (Munich, 1911). Venturi, *op. cit.*

3 A. Milanesi, *Documenti per la Storia dell'Arte Senese* (Siena, 1854). Pope-Hennessy, *op. cit.*, p. 177. P. Bacci, *Documenti Toscani per la Storia dell'Arte* (Florence, 1910).

4 C. Gnudi, *Nicola, Arnolfo, Lapo*. Carli, *op. cit.*

5 They are represented once previously on an eleventh-century mosaic. See G. H. & E. R. Crichton, *Nicola Pisano* (Cambridge, 1938), p. 85.

6 J. Huizinga, *The Waning of the Middle Ages* (Harmondsworth, Penguin Books, 1955), p. 203.

7 For the most cogent exposition of the relationship between High Scholasticism and the arts, see Panofsky, *Gothic Architecture and Scholasticism*.

8 The importance of Joachim and Joachimism is discussed by John Moorman, *The History of the Franciscan Order;* by Geoffrey Barraclough in *The Medieval Papacy* (London, Thames & Hudson, 1968); and by Norman Cohn in *The Pursuit of the Millennium* (London, Secker & Warburg, 1957). It will suffice to say here that towards the close of the twelfth century, Joachim da Fiore, a Calabrian abbot, had been inspired to proclaim in his interpretation of the Revelation of St John a messianic doctrine predicated on three ages: successively those of the Father (the Age of Law), the Son (the Age of the Gospels) and the Holy Ghost (the Age of the Culmination of Human History). This third stage, according to Joachim's numerous followers, was destined to begin in 1260 with the reign of Anti-Christ, a phase lasting three and a half years, to be followed by a millennium which would see a free community of perfected beings having replaced Church and Empire, living in harmony without benefit of clergy.

The doctrines of Joachim were treated with great seriousness throughout Italy and during his lifetime three popes urged him to write down his revelation. His prophecy was, however, condemned as heretical in 1256 but the half-century following his death saw the Spirituals foster the movement and add to its 'prophecies'. They identified 'the Emperor of the Last Days' with the Emperor Frederick II and despite the fact that he died in 1250, the prophecies continued to be believed for many years.

As a result, a series of commentaries and, in due

course, a body of wholly spurious writings were fathered on the long-dead Joachim and great efforts were made in the mid-fourteenth century to have him canonized. Among the spurious writings attributed to Joachim is one which I suspect is relevant to Giovanni Pisano for reasons which will presently emerge – the *Exposito Sibylla et Merlino*.

9 B. Berenson, *Piero della Francesca: the Ineloquent in Art* (London, Chapman & Hall, 1954).

10 Keller, *op. cit.*, maintains that it 'can be proved' that Giovanni went to France and that he went as an itinerant mason, but he does not produce his proofs.

11 Gordon Leff, *Paris and Oxford Universities in the 13th and 14th Centuries* (New York, Wiley, 1968).

12 Some scholars, notably R. Barsotti, 'Gli antichi inventari della cattedrale di Pisa', *Critica d'Arte*, IV (1957), give this sculpture a much later date.

13 J. Seznek, *The Survival of the Pagan Gods* (New York, Harper Bros., 1953), p. 128.

14 N. Fasola, *Nicola Pisano*, p. 70, states that the Perugia symbols may originally have stood on a separate column, like the Lion of St Mark in Venice. It is also possible that they postdate the Fountain, an argument partly based on the water piping adapted to the group which passes through the creatures' heads. Of the twelve protomes he accepts eight as original.

15 Giorgio Vasari, *Lives of the Most Eminent Painters, Sculptors and Architects* (London, Bohn, 1894): *Nicola and Giovanni of Pisa*. Vasari's list of works by both Nicola and Giovanni which had already been destroyed or have not since survived is as long and as sad as usual, and, as usual, although his work is as fundamental to the study of the Pisani as it is to the whole history of Italian art, it is not wholly accurate in detail.

16 Vasari, *op. cit.*

4 The First Sculptures for the Pisa Baptistry

1 The half-length carvings of Christ (Fig. *f*) and St Thomas from the west front of the Cathedral at Reims (now in the Musée Lapidaire) are comparable in size and probably in date. They measure 2.10 m. × 2 m.

2 Keller, *op. cit.*, p. 66.

3 Sigmund Freud, *Collected Papers*, IV (New York, Basic Books, 1959).

4 I have reproduced a drawing of my own to illustrate the mouth and chin of David from an angle from which it cannot be (or has not been) photographed and one from which it could never have been seen while it stood on the façade.

5 Herlihy in his *Pisa in the Early Renaissance* gives the losses at Meloria. They were huge. She lost seven galleys, thirty-three smaller ships, and nine thousand prisoners were taken. The dead were

uncounted. The battle took place at the mouth of the Arno, fifteen miles from the city.

5   THE DECADE AT SIENA

1   Vasari, *op. cit.*

2   P. Bacci, 'Documenti e Commenti per la Storia dell'Arte', in *Le Arti* IV (1941–42); he also discusses in detail the documents relating to Giovanni's activity in Siena.

3   E. Carli, *La Scultura Lignea Senese* (Milan, 1964), p. 130, pl. 10.

4   Harald Keller, *op. cit.*

5   P. Bacci, *op. cit.*, considers this an indication of Franco-Italian bonds among Giovanni's acquaintances.

6   This situation was not so uncommon as those who see medieval craftsmen through a romantic haze may suppose. Coulton (*op. cit.*, p. 484) speaks of a repetition of such complaints 'with wearisome emphasis', from the time of Berthold of Regensburg to that of S. Antonius of Florence, on the subject of the guile, idleness and shoddy workmanship of artisans, except under the strictest supervision.

7   John White, *op. cit.*

8   *Ibid.*, p. 72.

6   THE SIENA CATHEDRAL FAÇADE:
THE IVORIES AND WOOD CARVINGS

1   The original arrangement of the statues on the façade is convincingly proposed by Keller in 'Die Bauplastik des Sieneser Doms', *Kunstgesch. Jahrb. des Biblioteca Hertziana* I (1937); their re-arrangement on the façade by Lusini in *Il Duomo di Siena* (1911).

2   Carli describes the condition of the statues after their removal from the façade in 'Giovanni Pisano a Siena', *Acts of the 20th International Congress of the History of Art – Romanesque and Gothic* (Princeton, 1963).

3   J. Pope-Hennessy, 'New Works by Giovanni Pisano, I', in his *Essays in Italian Sculpture* (London, Phaidon, 1968).

4   Andrew Martindale in a review of John White's *Art and Architecture in Italy, 1250–1400*, in *Burlington Magazine*, Sept. 1967.

5   G. G. Coulton, *The Fate of Medieval Art*, Part II, p. 375.

6   It is this dual role, the mother and child as Mary and Christ at one and the same time, which Moore has described himself as seeking to express in his Northampton Madonna. He felt that the divine and the human must coexist in a sacred image without one role being sacrificed wholly to the other.

7   John White, *op. cit.*, maintains that this was so intended.

8   Pope-Hennessy, *op. cit.*

9   R. Barsotti in *Critica d'Arte* IV (1957).

10 Ragghianti, 'La Madonna eburnea di Giovanni Pisano', *Critica d'Arte* I (1954), discusses the condition of the ivory.

11 Barsotti, *op. cit.*, discusses the documents relating to the ivory in *Nuovi studi sulla Madonna eburnea di Giovanni Pisano*, pp. 47–56, and 'Gli antichi inventari . . .' (*op. cit.*), p. 161.

12 Pope-Hennessy, *op. cit.*

7   THE RETURN TO PISA AND THE PISTOIA PULPIT

1   D. Herlihy, *Mediaeval and Renaissance Pistoia* (Yale, 1967), who also remarks the great growth of artisan industries, especially stone and wood-workers, after 1296.

2   Some indication of the situation may be deduced from the fact that during Giovanni's lifetime there were at least fifteen pontificates, thirteen of them between 1261 and 1305. When temporal politics determine policy there is a tendency to elect compromise popes with a short expectancy of life.

3   Edgar Wind, *Michelangelo's Prophets and Sibyls*. The Proceedings of the British Academy, Vol. VI (London, O.U.P., 1960).

4 Wind, *op. cit.*

5 E. Carli in *Il Pulpito di Siena* reproduces two unidentified sibyls in a spandrel (pls. 93 *a* and *b*) and also the Hebrew sibyl 'Sabbe', with Solomon, whom she visited and to whom she foretold the Advent (pls. 94 and 95).

That Nicola confined his sibyls within the constricted area of the spandrel, whereas Giovanni gave them more important positions as angle figures on his pulpits and as monumental sculpture on the Siena Cathedral façade, seems to argue that the sibyl had achieved a far greater significance to him than she had for his father.

6 Seznek, *The Survival of the Pagan Gods*, p. 123.

7 Bacci's reconstruction of the Pisa Cathedral pulpit as it now stands places eight sibyls at the angles of the spandrels. Géza Jászai's hypothesis in *Die Pisaner Domkanzel* (Munich, 1968), asserts that the pulpit in its original form represented the ten sibyls cited by Lactantius. To these, two more were added, and were depicted in a now lost fresco cycle commissioned by Cardinal Giovanni Orsini and referred to by Wind, *op. cit.*, p. 52. These frescoes are mentioned by Poggio and other contemporaries.

On the other hand, Michelangelo depicted only five sibyls on the Sistine Chapel ceiling and ten are among the fifteenth- and sixteenth-century intarsia on the floor of Siena Cathedral. There, however, the number is increased from nine by the inclusion of two separate versions of the Cumaean Sibyl, one by Giovanni di Stefano and one by Vito di Marco.

8 Bard Thompson, *Patristic Use of the Sibylline Oracles* XIII (Oxford, 1952).

9 In Caxton's translation of the *Legenda Aurea* we learn that the Emperor Octavian (who would become Augustus) sent for a prophetess 'named Sibyl for to demand of her if there were any so great and like him in the earth or if any should come after him'. The Sibyl gazed at the sun and there saw revealed 'a maid holding a child'. This she showed the Emperor who accepted the vision, whereupon 'The Christian men made a church of the same chamber of the Emperor and named it Ara Coeli' and as late as 1251 a mosaic by Cavallini is there said to have represented Augustus and the Sibyl together.

However, this Sibyl was thought to be the Erythraean – the archsibyl so to speak – and also the Tiburtine, as she appears in the late thirteenth-century *Cronica Tributorum* in the form of a golden-haired virgin. She is also, as a result of her prophecy of Christianity to come, asserted to speak of it in Virgil's 4th Eclogue, and Servius, the principal medieval commentator on Virgil, confused her with the Sibyl of Cumae from whom Aeneas in the Aeneid Book VI learned the whereabouts of the Golden Bough.

Lactantius and Augustine give the Trojan Cassandra, the Delphic Pythia and the Cumaean Sibyl the foremost place among those involved and evolving oracles, and Lactantius supposed almost every Christian belief to be corroborated by a Sibylline utterance. To all this was added, in a pseudo-Augustinian document called *Contra Judaeos, Paganes et Arianos Sermio de Symbolo*, a Hebrew sibyl variously named Sabbe and Sambethe who promises the Advent just as Virgil's sibyl in the 4th Eclogue promises the Last Judgement. This Hebrew sibyl is also identified with the Persian or Babylonian; Josephus, who refers to her only once (as Sibyllina) makes her not the sister of Moses, as tradition suggests she was called in Giovanni's marble of her on the Siena Cathedral façade, but Moses' daughter-in-law. She it is who appears in a spandrel of Nicola's Siena pulpit.

As a witness to Gospel truth, Justin Martyr, in his 'Exhortation to the Greeks', cited her verification six times and Clement of Alexandria quoted 'the Sibyl' eleven times, while Augustine pondered her admission to the City of God when considering her acrostic in Book VIII and made her Erythraean and contemporary of the siege of Troy (and therefore of Cassandra).

Inevitably such a plethora was meat for fabulists, from such sober and diverse opinion as that of Isidore of Seville who states that all prophetesses were called 'sibyls' in Greek, to Bernard of Morval, who is precise, in his apocalyptic *De Contemptu Mundi*, in stating that she prophesied the reign of anti-Christ, born of the tribe of Dan, and foresaw that the 'Great Emperor' would offer his crown to Almighty God at Jerusalem.

10 W. L. Kinter & J. R. Keller, *The Sibyl* (Philadelphia, Dorrance & Co., 1967).

11 Moorman, *The History of the Franciscan Order*, p. 268.

12 Wind, *op. cit.*, p. 62.

13 John White, *Art and Architecture in Italy*, p. 72.

14 Kinter & Keller, *op. cit.*, pp. 36, 37.

8 THE PISA PULPIT

1 The inscription runs:

> IN NOMINE DOMINE AMEN
> BORGHOGNO DI TADO FE
> CE FARE LO PERBIO NVOV
> O LO QUALE E' IN DUOMO
> COMINCIOSI CORENTE ANI
> DOMINI MCCCII FU FINIT
> O IN ANI DOMINI CORENT
> E MCCCXI DEL MESE D
> IICIENMBRE.

(In the name of the Lord, Amen. Burgundio di Tado had this new pulpit made. It is located in the cathedral [and was] begun in the year 1302 and finished in 1311 in the month of December.)

2 D. Herlihy, *Pisa in the Early Renaissance*, p. 119, describes the rise of the Falcone family. Its head, in 1301, was Iohannes, 'consul of the sea', a dignitary of the *curia maris*. Nello and Montefeltro are discussed in the Plate Notes, p. 225, in relation to the two 'portraits' set between the Evangelists on a support of the Pisa pulpit.

3 Jászai, *Die Pisaner Domkanzel*.

4 Both Toesca in *Il Trecento* (1951), p. 246, and Weinberger in *Burlington Magazine* LXX (1937), pp. 59–60, discuss these lapses.

5 Toesca assumes that the first words should be taken literally to refer to Giovanni's travels abroad, whereas Bacci takes them to be metaphorical, meaning the circumscribing of the four parts of the world separated by the four rivers (the Evangelists) in the design of the work.

6 See Bacci, *op. cit.*, Jászai, *op. cit.*, and a summary of their views in the Plate Notes, pp. 223–6. See also Bacci, *La Ricostruzione del Pergamo di Giovanni Pisano nel Duomo di Pisa* (Milan & Rome, 1926).

7 White, *op. cit.*, pp. 83, 87.

9 THE LAST SCULPTURES

1 Vasari, *op. cit.*, notes that Giovanni visited Florence expressly to view Arnolfo's work on the Cathedral and meet Giotto, 'of whom he had heard great things related . . .' No exact date is given but the visit is assumed to have been in the 1290's. I see no reason to discount this statement.

2 The fifteenth-century Roncioni MS. Also quoted by Vasari.

3 Both the Madonna and the head of 'Pisa' were discovered by W. Weinberger and first published by him. *The Burlington Magazine* LXX (1937).

4 C. Marcenaro, 'La Madonna della tomba di Margherita di Brabante', *Paragone* No. 167 (1963). See also 'Per la tomba di Margherita di Brabante', *Paragone* No. 133 (1961).

5 W. R. Valentiner, *Tino da Camaino* (Paris, 1935), p. 43.

6 Max Seidel, 'Ein neu entdecktes Fragment des Genoeser Grabmals der Königin Margarethe von Giovanni Pisano', *Pantheon* XXVI. 5 (Sept./Oct. 1968), pp. 335–51).

7 M. Seidel. *Pantheon. op. cit.*

8 Dr Marcenaro believes the Madonna for the tomb of Margaret to post-date the Madonna della Cintola.

Dimensions of statues are given thus:
height × width × depth

The Perugia Fountain

COMPLETED in 1278, the Fontana Maggiore **(1–14)** stands in the main square of Perugia beside the cathedral.

Plans for a fountain to supply the centre of the city had long been contemplated and discussion in the Consiglio for the provision of an aqueduct to carry water from Monte Pacciano, a distance of some three miles, were documented in 1254 and in 1262. In 1276 deliberations were renewed on the 5th and 8th of May and the documents extant cover the period from those dates until August 1277. In that year the hydraulics engineer Boninsegna was brought from Orvieto and set to work to complete the reconstruction and enlargement of the existing aqueduct. Placed apparently under the authority of the Benedictine Fra Bevegnato (described as *Benvegnate bonus – sapientis ad omnia pronus* in the inscription on the superior basin), Boninsegna (concerning whom the inscription reads: *Ingenio clarum ductorem scimus aquarum | qui Boninsegna vulgatur mente benigna*) seems likely to have contributed to the construction. In this same inscription Nicola and Giovanni are named between Bevegnato and Boninsegna in the following terms:

NOMINA SCULPTORUM   FONTIS SUNT ISTA BONORUM
(ARTE CELEB)RATUS   NICOLAUS AD (OMNIA GR)ATUS
EST FLOS SCULPTORUM   GRATISSIMUS ISQUE
                                        PROBORUM:
EST GENITOR PRIMUS   GENITUS CARISSIMUS IMUS
CUI SI NON DAMPNES   NOMEN DIC ESSE IOHANNES
NATU PISANI   SINT MULTO TEMPORE SANI

On the inferior basin, above a panel representing two superb eagles in relief **(62, 63)**, a further inscription refers to Giovanni alone. This reads: *Boni Iohannes (est) sculptor hujus operis* (Giovanni is the sculptor of this good work) which has been taken to mean that he carved this particular panel or alternatively that he was responsible under Nicola for the entire corpus of the sculpture on the fountain. The design of the edifice is related to Nicola's pulpits and the upper inscription, of which the Latin is given above, states: 'The names of the good sculptors of the fountain are these: Nicola, much honoured and to whom all are grateful (who) is the flower of sculptors: progenitor of a most dear son whose name is Giovanni, born of the Pisans; may they be much preserved in health.' This argues that Nicola had primacy over the total work. Opinion is much divided as to the division of hands in the execution of all parts of the work, but the speed with which it went forward suggests a large and well disciplined workshop.

The fountain is in three tiers, but may have been designed in four, the water at one time falling from a small bronze basin, now lost, which was supported by the bronze group of caryatids known as the *Water Carriers* **(2, 3)**. This group was cast in bronze and inscribed by a founder named 'Rubeus'. Until Fasola's restoration in 1948–49, a further group consisting of bronze lions and griffins **(12, 13)** rose above the Water Carriers, but this has now been removed to the museum of Perugia on the grounds that the piping for this group appears to have been extemporized, indicating therefore that the splendid creatures were not designed for the fountain. It has been suggested that they were intended to stand upon a separate column as does the Lion of St Mark in Venice. Whatever its original purpose, the vigour and quality of this group strongly suggest Giovanni's work.

The bronze basin from which the Water Carriers rise is supported by a single hollow column, through which the water is piped, and this column, in turn, stands in a marble basin with twelve convex sides. At each of the angles and at the centre of each curving, unsculptured face, stands a statue. From the bases of the twelve angles jut bronze animal protomes **(4–11)**, eight of which are original in Fasola's opinion. These are:

The Lion
4
The Leopard
5
The Wolf
6
The Female Wolf
7
The Gazelle
8
The Horse
9
The Bull
10
The Boar
11

Below this basin, which is supported by a central polygonal column and fifty-eight alternating subsidiary supports in the form of columnar and octagonal pillars with foliate capitals, the lowest and largest marble basin is a polygon of twenty-five sides.

The statues on the superior marble basin represent symbolic personifications of cities and institutions and representations of civic dignitaries together with biblical and mythological figures, saints and ecclesiastics. All these are relevant in one way or another to Perugia and her history.

In sequence they are:

The City of Chiusi
16
Inscribed *Domina Clu(s)ii – Ferens Granum Perusie*

The City of Perugia
17
Inscribed *Augusta Perusia Fertilis de omnibus his*

Lake Trasimeno
18
Inscribed *Domina Laci – Ferens Pisces Perusie*

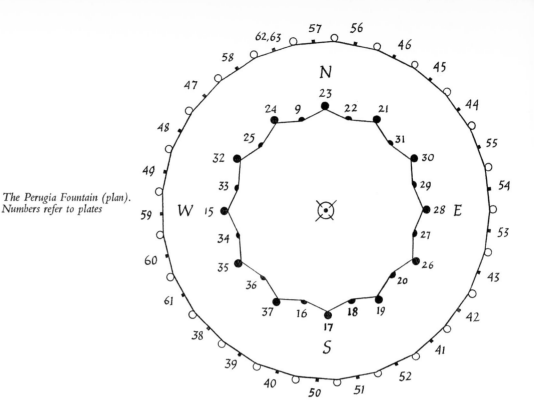

The Perugia Fountain (plan).
Numbers refer to plates

St Herculanus
19
Inscribed *Sanctus Erculanus – Pastor Perusinorum*

The Cleric of Herculanus
20
Inscribed *Clericus Proditor – Sancti Herculani*
This figure is also called *Il Chierico Traditore* and represents a young priest who, during the siege of Perugia by Totila, opened the gate to the enemy.

St Benedict
26
Inscribed *Sanctus Benedictus*

St John the Baptist
27
Inscribed *Ecce Agnus Dei*

Solomon
28
Inscribed *Rex – Salomon*
This sculpture is very much weathered.

David
29
Inscribed *David – Habens spiritum Prophekie*

Salome with the head of the Baptist

30

Inscribed *Puella Ferens – Rex*

The meaning of this inscription is obscure and it may be incomplete.

Moses

31

Inscribed *Moyses – Cum virga Et Lege*

Matteo di Correggio (the Podestà of Perugia)

21

Inscribed *Nobilis miles – Matheus De Corigia*

St Michael

22

Inscribed *Angelus Munitus – No ilis*

Aulestes

23

Inscribed *Heulixstes Peru – Sine Conditor Urbis*

The Trojan hero, legendary founder of Perugia and King of Etruria.

Ernano di Sasseferrato

24

Inscribed *Nobilis Miles Dominus – Hermanus De Sas Ferato*

Capitano del Popolo of Perugia at the time when the fountain was built. With Matteo del Correggio, he is named in the deliberations of the Consiglio on 14 January 1278.

Victory

25

Inscribed *Victoria – Magna*

A symbol of the triumph of the Guelph party over the Ghibellines.

St Peter

32

Inscribed *Sanctus Petrus – Apostolus*

The Church of Rome

33

Inscribed *Eclesia – Romana*

The face of this figure is modern.

The City of Rome

15

Inscribed *Roma – Caput Mundi*

The weathered original is now in the museum and is replaced on the fountain by a copy.

Theologia

34

Inscribed *Divinitas – Excelsa*

St Paul

35

Inscribed *Sanctus Paulus – Doctor Gentium*

The Cleric of St Laurence

36

Inscribed *Clericus – Beati Laurenti*

St Laurence

37

Inscribed *Sanctus Laurentius – Bonum Opus Operatus est*

The figure of Melchisedek, which should stand between Eulistes (**23**) and Ernano di Sasseferrato (**24**) is lost and is replaced on the fountain by a modern statue.

The lower marble basin displays fifty upright low reliefs in pairs on its twenty-five faces. Each face is divided from its neighbour by three spiral columns of a type related to the angle columns of the Pisa Baptistry Pulpit.

The reliefs on the lower basin represent:

January

38

Inscribed *Januarius – Uxor*

February
39
Inscribed *Februarius – Sotius*

March
40
Inscribed *Marcius – Socius*

April
50
Inscribed *Aprelis – Uxor*

May
51
Inscribed *Madius – Uxor*

June
52
Inscribed *Junius*

July
41
Inscribed *Julius – Sozius*

August
42
Inscribed *Agus(t)u – Uxor*

September
43
Inscribed *September – Socius*

October
53
Inscribed *O(c)tober – Socius*

November
54
Inscribed *November – Sotius*

December
55
Inscribed *December – Socius*

The use of the terms *Socius* (variously *Sotius* and *Sozius*) and *Uxor* accentuates the unity of the diptychs of the months, since in popular writing of the time they designate man and wife. The activities characteristic of each month are sometimes portrayed sequentially as in *June*, where a peasant harvests a sheaf of corn and then, in the companion panel, threshes the grain; sometimes allegorically, as Spring is represented in *April* by a boy holding a flowering branch and a woman who bears a cornucopia and a basket of fruit. Sometimes both sections of a panel constitute a single scene as when man and wife feast by the fire in *January* or nobles go hawking in *May*. The signs of the Zodiac, which appear in each month, derive from a tradition which originated in Roman art and was widely popular during the Middle Ages. The signs, apart from any more esoteric meaning, performed the function of a calendar for those who could not read.

The Labours of the Months are divided from those representing the Eight Liberal Arts by a panel which bears the Lion, and its companion the Griffin, as symbols of Perugia **(44)**.

The Liberal Arts are represented in some cases by different attributes from those which appear at the base of the central column of Nicola's Siena Pulpit and on the fountain the personifications of Rhetoric, Arithmetic and Grammar are accompanied by pupils. Not only are the personifications more elaborate but as sculpture the reliefs are far superior to the series at Siena. They represent:

Grammar – Dialectic
45
Inscribed *Gramatica – Dialectica*

Rhetoric – Arithmetic
46
Inscribed *Rectorica – Arismetrica*

Geometry – Music
56
Inscribed *Geometria – Musica*

Astrology – Philosophy
57
Inscribed *Astrolomia – Fylosofia*

The Liberal Arts are divided from the Scenes from Sacred History, Proverbs and Scenes from Roman History by the two eagles **(62, 63)** which bear the inscription naming Giovanni as sculptor. The Biblical Scenes and Proverbs represent:

The Fall and Expulsion from Eden
58
Inscribed *Eva decepit Adam – Eva Fec(it) me Peccare*

Samson and the Lion and Samson and Delilah
47
Inscribed *Sanson Fortis – Sanson et Dalida*

A morality showing a lion beneath a flowering tree and a man beating a lion cub (?)
48
Inscribed *Si Vis Ut Timeat Leo – Verbera c( )tulum*
The exact meaning both of the inscription and of the images portrayed on this panel is obscure. It has been suggested that the morality depends from the proposition that fear of the grown lion does not prevent man from tormenting its child and thus the animals inferior to sinful man suffer under and revolt from his wickedness.

David and Goliath
49
Inscribed *D(a)vit – Golia*

Ancient history is illustrated in the two succeeding panels, the first of which shows Romulus and Remus **(59)**. The second **(60)** shows them suckled by the wolf on the left of the panel and on the right a woman with a birdcage. The inscription above the left-hand panel reads *Lupa que nutrivit Romulum et Remulum (Mater Romuli);* the inscription above the second half of the panel is lost, but the woman may represent the goddess Rhea Silva in her capacity of Patroness of Rome. This panel is much weathered and is now in the Perugia Museum. It is replaced by a copy on the fountain.

The ultimate panel in the sequence on the lower basin portrays two further moralities in the form of fables from Aesop: the Wolf and the Stork, and the Wolf and the Sheep. They are inscribed *Quando grus evulsit os De Gutture Lupi – Quando Lupus comedit Angnum sine causa* **(61)**.

The fountain has frequently been restored during its history. It suffered damage in 1349, was apparently restored incorrectly in 1474, received further minor restorations in 1858 and was completely dismantled, restored and reassembled in 1948–49. The measurements, transliteration of abbreviated Latin inscriptions and details of the construction are taken from *La Fontana di Perugia* by Giusta Nicco Fasola and Francesco Santi (Rome, 1951), who were responsible for the 1948–49 restoration. Dr Fasola includes the texts of the historical documents relating to the fountain, the complete surviving inscriptions and also extensive iconographic information in his plate notes. Among books by other authors dealing with the fountain are: G.H. & E.R. Crichton, *Nicola Pisano and the Revival of Sculpture in Italy* (Cambridge 1938), Chapter IV, and Kathrin Hoffmann Curtius, *Das Programm der Fontana Maggiore in Perugia* (Düsseldorf, 1968).

Measurements: Diptych panels of the inferior basin, 0.69 × 0.97 m. Statues on the upper basin (average height), 0.75 to 0.78 m. Bronze group of Water Carriers (height), 1.25 m. Diameter of bronze basin, 2.15 m. Internal column, 1.40 m.

The External Decoration
of the Pisa Baptistry

THE SCULPTURE illustrated in this section falls into two distinct groups. The first sixteen illustrations show marbles carved between 1278 and Giovanni's departure for Siena in or before 1285. During the first years of this period, Nicola was alive, although probably an old, perhaps a very old man. The situation is further complicated by the possibility that Nicola had begun work on the external decoration of the Baptistry between the completion of his Pisa Baptistry pulpit in 1260 and the Siena commission of 1265. Nothing is known of the nature of his contribution to the Baptistry sculptures in those years. His work may have been entirely architectural. It is, however, just possible that the three busts of the *Salvator Mundi* **(67)**, the *St John the Baptist (?)* **(68)** and the *Annunciate (?) Madonna* **(69** and **70)** were carved by Nicola as early as 1265. They are usually dated 1280–84 and they seem to me to have something of Giovanni's urgency which suggests a greater degree of collaboration between father and son than the early date would permit. The three busts were removed from above the east portal and placed in the museum in 1846.

Nicola returned to Pisa after the completion of the Perugia fountain and Vasari maintained that he was a very old man by then. There is absolute documentary silence concerning Giovanni between 1278 and 1284 and it is in those years, or part of them, that he may have visited France. There is, however, no real evidence as to his whereabouts. We are therefore left with a group of nine huge high-relief carvings which are not busts of that Apulian type which shows the half-length figure and which had been evolved to decorate the buildings and, in particular, the Capuan Gate of the Emperor Frederick. This type Nicola could have brought with him in his repertoire from the south. But the nine colossal high-relief figures are two-

third or three-quarter length, ending at the lap, an entirely new development in Italian and certainly in Tuscan sculpture at this period.

If the three busts **(67–70)** are to be attributed to Nicola, with or without Giovanni's greater or lesser collaboration, the great Madonna and Child **(64–66)**, the Four Evangelists **(71–74)** and the Four Prophets **(75–79)** are likely to have been either a collaboration between father and son in which the son played an active role, or wholly controlled by Giovanni, if not entirely carved by him alone.

Expert opinion is divided in the matter of attributions and among the authorities named here, a majority ascribe the figures, thought to have been carved before 1284, to Nicola and his workshop. If, however, Giovanni was at Pisa for any length of time between 1278 and 1284, who but he is likely to have dominated the workshop in view of the almost equal partnership between father and son which is suggested by the Perugia Fountain inscriptions?

Among those who divide the work of this phase between Nicola and Giovanni, Venturi gives the bust of St John the Baptist **(68)** and Pope-Hennessy gives the Prophets and Evangelists **(71–79)** to Giovanni. Pope-Hennessy also suggests that the great Madonna and Child **(64–66)** may have been Nicola's last work. If this is so, it was an extraordinary physical achievement for a man in or nearing his eighties and, in these terms, comparable only to Michelangelo's final sculpture. Since no other carving of comparable size from Nicola's hand survives, the whole division of work on these vast sculptures must remain conjectural.

Marangoni considers that the busts are earlier than the large Baptistry figures, that Giovanni worked on the architecture of the tabernacles between 1278 and 1284 and that if Giovanni also worked on the great high-relief figures, without Nicola's collaboration, they are his earliest attributable works.

This group of nine sculptures was removed from the façade of the Baptistry in 1947 and has been placed inside the building. The niches they occupied have either been left empty (see **92)** or contain reproductions. Because of the position the figures were destined to occupy, they were carved to be seen from one frontal position only and they are of a relief high enough to have given the impression, in their setting, of being carved in the round. Some of them are deeply hollowed out from behind, notably the St John, some, like the unidentified prophet **(77)** are not.

It has been generally acknowledged that Giovanni's first fully independent freestanding sculpture is the half-length high-relief of the Madonna **(149)** which Keller dates at 1275 (although this early dating has been questioned). This, too, is a three-quarter-length figure, made so by the addition of a separate section, probably carved later than the upper part of the sculpture. If this was Giovanni's idea and it was new to monumental Italian sculpture, then it is arguable that the unusual length of the Baptistry figures is related to this innovation. The additional height which it gave to the figure would be of advantage when it was viewed from below and this would have been even more valuable in the case of the Baptistry Façade where the figures in their niches stood at a great height from the spectator.

The busts and reliefs from the earlier phase of the Baptistry decoration represent:

The Madonna and Child
Details **64, 65, 66.** Cat. **191**
184 × 90 × 70.25 cms.
In the interior of the Baptistry

The Salvator Mundi
67. Cat **192**
92.5 × 63 × 43.2 cms.
In the Museo San Matteo, Pisa

St John the Baptist (?)
68. Cat. **193**
92 × 54.5 × 41.2 cms.
In the Museo San Matteo, Pisa

The Madonna Annunciate (?)
69. Detail **70.** Cat. **194**
77.5 × 71 × 53.25 cms.
In the Museo San Matteo, Pisa

St Matthew the Evangelist
71. Cat. **195**
173 × 103 × 43 cms.
In the interior of the Baptistry

St Mark the Evangelist
72. Cat. **196**
170 × 92 × 41 cms.
In the interior of the Baptistry

St Luke the Evangelist
73. Cat. **197**
178 × 102 × 51 cms.
In the interior of the Baptistry

St John the Evangelist
74. Cat. **198**
187 × 115.25 × 46 cms.
In the interior of the Baptistry

David
75. Cat. **199**
165 × 94 × 48 cms.
In the interior of the Baptistry

Moses
76. Cat. **200**
189.75 × 106 × 43.5 cms.
In the interior of the Baptistry

An Unidentified Prophet
77. Cat. **201**
169 × 88 × 54.5 cms.
In the interior of the Baptistry

An Unidentified Prophet
78, 79. Cat. **202**
165 × 72.5 × 56 cms.
In the interior of the Baptistry

The second phase of Giovanni's external decoration of the Baptistry was in the main carried out after his return from Siena in 1297–98, although he was briefly at Pisa in 1295. Various undertakings connected him with the cathedral authorities during those years, of which the largest required a series of over-lifesize carvings of single figures in the round to surmount the tabernacles containing the large relief figures already discussed. Twenty-one of these pinnacle figures by Giovanni and his workshop are now in the Museo San Matteo at Pisa in various degrees of preservation, but all of them, being of the friable marble of San Giuliano, are severely weathered. Of these twenty-one, eight are, in varying degrees, masterpieces and four are among Giovanni's highest achievements. The others are of uneven quality and in some cases so worn as to be barely decipherable. Many of these appear to be the work of inferior assistants.

It is impossible to establish with certainty what any of the figures was intended to represent in iconographic terms, but several are referred to in the museum as 'dancing', one is called 'Salome' and the best-preserved male figure is called a *Santo Guerrero* or holy warrior.

The pinnacle sculptures illustrated here are:

Female figure with a high headdress
80, 81. Detail of head **82.** Cat. **203**
158 × 64.75 × 38 cms.
She is craning forward and holding her skirt taut below her breasts. (A sibyl?)

Headless female figure
83. Detail **84.** Cat. **204**
123.2 × 21.75 × 18.5 cms.
She is swaying backwards from the waist, and holding her skirt on her left hip. (sibyl?)

Warrior drawing his sword
85. Cat. **205**
109 × 43.75 × 37 cms.

Female figure holding a round object
86. Cat. **206**
162 × 50.8 × 45.75 cms.
Salome with the head of John the Baptist?

Headless female figure holding a jar
87, 88. Cat. **207**
121 × 45.1 × 36 cms.

Headless female figure holding a scroll
89. Cat. **208**
135 × 38.75 × 34.5 cms.

Female figure
90. Detail **91.** Cat. **209**
145 × 43.75 × 50 cms.
She is twisting and inclining forward, holding a scroll

Female figure
Cat. **210**
159.2 × 48.5 × 33 cms.
She is turning, with right hand on her breast and left hand holding her skirt. The forehead is missing

Detail of the upper part of the Pisa Baptistry showing the tier of triangular tabernacles over the colonnade
92
The nine colossal statues now inside the Baptistry occupied the niches in these tabernacles, the great Madonna being set over the principal door. The Pinnacle figures, reproductions of which may be seen in this plate, surmounted the tabernacles.

The Siena Cathedral Façade

THE UNADORNED FAÇADE of the cathedral was completed in 1284. From that year, or soon after, Giovanni was principally occupied with contributing both as sculptor and as architect to the decoration of the façade, but there is no precise documentary information concerning either his plans or the individual sculptures for which he was responsible. As the façade stands today, nothing for which Giovanni is believed to have been responsible exists above the portal zone and the only sculpture still *in situ*, apart from decorative details of the portals (Cat. **231**), is one half figure of a horse emerging from above a pilaster at the level of the tympana of the principal doors **(106)**. It is situated at the north turret and was balanced by another, the remains of which are now in the Museum of the Cathedral (Cat. **227**). Between the horses, half-length figures of a bull **(107** and **109**. Plate 107 is taken from a photograph of the modern copy, to show it as it was *in situ*), two lions and a griffin also jutted from the façade in a symbolical relationship which remains obscure. Immediately above the siting of these animal sculptures, a ledge runs across the façade, turning at each end along the flanks of the twin towers. This ledge, interrupted by the tympana of the three doors, was the setting for the fourteen freestanding figures of prophets and sibyls which are Giovanni Pisano's most celebrated contribution to monumental sculpture. Today all that remains of these fourteen figures are in the Cathedral Museum at Siena, with one exception – the fragment of the prophet Haggai, now in the Victoria & Albert Museum in London **(101**. Cat. **212)**.

From the sixteenth century on, these figures were renovated at different periods and were shifted about on the façade. If it were not for inscriptions carved on the façade itself, Giovanni's intended arrangement of the figures and their subtle rhythmic interplay as a sculptural complex could not even be reconstructed in the mind. As it is, the figures ranged in the museum are not in the relationship we may assume that Giovanni intended. They were originally designed in such a way as to balance one another across the façade, and with the exception of Plato **(97** and **102)** at the northern end of the front and Habakkuk **(100**. Cat. **222)**, who balanced Plato at the southern end, both of whom are speaking outwards, each figure is in converse with its neighbour. Thus, on Plato's right, Daniel (?) a figure so mutilated as to be devoid of all original work save for part of his torso (Cat. **216**) discoursed with the Erythraean (?) Sibyl **(95**. Cat. **217)**. Then, separated from their neighbours and from each other by the tympana of the great doors, David **(105**. Cat. **218)** spoke with Solomon **(99**. Cat. **219)**. At the southern end, Moses **(98**. Cat. **220)** conferred with Joshua (Cat. **221**), turning from Habakkuk on his right. On the north flank of the façade, Balaam **(103**. Cat. **214)**, Isaiah **(96**. Cat. **213)** and Haggai **(101**. Cat. **212)** in colloquy, were balanced on the south by Simeon **(104**. Cat. **223)** in discourse with Miriam (or Mary of Moses) **(93, 94**. Cat. **224)** and Aristotle (Cat. **225**), a figure scarcely less mutilated than that of Daniel.

The work was not erected whilst Giovanni was in Siena and some of it may have been incomplete when he left. Without documentary evidence, the sequence in which the sculptures were carved may be deduced from a comparison with his earlier work on the angle statues on the Perugia Fountain and the large high-relief figures for the Pisa Baptistry. From these it may be argued that the more compact and least radically articulated figures, such as the Erythraean Sibyl, Joshua, Plato and Habakkuk, preceded Solomon, David, Simeon and Moses in execution, but the order in which the individual figures were carved is unknown. The most radical in development, in its extraordinary articulation and distortion of human anatomy for sculptural ends, is the 'Mary of Moses', whose elongated neck and urgently expressive head are shown in detail in the frontispiece of this book. Comparable both in action and, putatively, in date to the most complete of the pinnacle figures for the Pisa Baptistry (80–82), these twisting figures are two of the most inspired inventions in Giovanni's canon. That they are both the work of the 1290's may be deduced from their resemblance to the sibyls on the Pistoia pulpit, carved in the following decade.

On the façade of the cathedral, the prophets and sibyls are reproduced in facsimile. Such is the condition of the originals in the museum that it has seemed advisable to give priority in the main plates to those figures and details of figures which are best preserved. Others, as well as different views of those reproduced in this section, will be found in the catalogue, together with photographs of certain of the figures as they looked before they were removed from the façade (107. Cat. 211 and 214).

Miriam or Mary, sister of Moses (a sibyl?)
94. Detail of head, frontispiece, 93. Cat. 224
189 × 68 × 64.75 cms.
In good condition. There are incipient horizontal fractures in the stone.

David
105. Cat. 218
193 × 68 × 36 cms.
Much weathered, the forehead and crown of head severely damaged and the fingers, lower lip, beard, right upper arm and shoulder blade restored.

Isaiah
96. Cat. 213
192 × 66 × 52.5 cms.
Much weathered; the hands and top of the scroll are restored and the statue is repaired below the knees.

Plato
97. Detail of head 102. Cat. 215
188 × 74 × 57 cms.
Much weathered; the right hand is damaged and the lower section of the robe restored.

Moses
98. Cat. 220
198 × 82.5 × 48 cms.
Much re-cut; the hands and scroll and the base below the shins are restored; the whole statue appears to have been painted grey.

Solomon
99. Cat. 219
184 × 59.5 × 51.5 cms.
Much weathered; both hands and the base have been restored and the scroll has been re-cut.

Habakkuk
Detail of head 100. Cat. 222
188 × 79 × 49 cms.
Much weathered, but the condition is otherwise good. The base is restored.

Haggai
Detail of head 101. Cat. 212
63.8 × 61 × 41 cms.
Fragment: in the Victoria & Albert Museum. The figure has been broken diagonally beneath the shoulders and the remainder is in Siena but not on view. There is some evidence of cutting at the base of the fragment.

Balaam
Detail of head 103. Cat. 214
189 × 87 × 47.5 cms.
One of the most severely damaged and restored figures, the Balaam is held together with iron clamps. The fractures in the stone are largely vertical. One hand, the nose, and the lower part of the figure restored. Unlike the other figures, apart from the Sibyl, the Balaam is not wholly hollowed out at the back, but only in one narrow section behind the right shoulder.

Simeon
Detail 104. Cat. 223
190 × 83 × 46.5 cms.

The head is re-cut; the base and sections of the drapery are restored and the whole appears to be coated with grey paint.

The Sibyl
95. Cat. **217**
190 × 64.5 × 52.5 cms.
The head appears re-cut and reduced (?). The base below the knees is restored and vertical fractures are repaired with iron clamps between right hand and base. Unlike the other figures, the Sibyl is a carving in the round.

Joshua
Cat. **221**
178 × 70 × 50 cms.
Much weathered; the crown is damaged; the right temple, mouth, chin and the base are restored.

Daniel (?)
Cat. **216**
Not exhibited in the museum, and so incomplete that measurements would be without meaning.

Aristotle
Cat. **225**
184 × 85.5 × 49.5 cms.
The head is a seventeenth-century restoration. Parts of the body and scroll are original, but incorrectly reorientated. Two large sections are broken away between the knees and the base.

Half Figure of a Horse
106. Cat. **226**
In situ on the façade. Measurements unavailable, but comparable in diemensions with its companion (Cat. 227). Keller states that the right knee and both hooves are restored.

Half Figure of a Horse
Cat. **227**
144 × 42.75 × 121 cms.

Head and right foreleg missing; the rest much damaged.

Half Figure of a Bull
109. As it appeared on the façade **107.** Cat. **228**
118 × 54 × 92.75 cms.
Much repaired with plaster of paris; overpainted.

Half Figure of a Lion
Cat. **229**
115 × 46 × 118.5 cms.
Severely damaged; face and right forepaw missing.

Wolf, with the Infants Romulus and Remus
108. Cat. **230**
64 × 170 × 43 cms.
The legs of the Wolf are damaged and all but the right foreleg (repaired) are incomplete. The Wolf was not part of the Cathedral façade, but would seem to have surmounted a separate freestanding column. It was a symbol of the city of Siena and may have stood in the square near the Palazzo Pubblico or elsewhere in the city.

The Façade of Siena Cathedral
110

The Siena façade has received more detailed attention from scholars than the Pisa Baptistry sculpture. On the façade, in general, see V. Lusini, *Il Duomo di Siena* (Siena, 1911), with special reference to the original disposition of the sculptures and the inscriptions on their scrolls; see also Keller, 'Die Bauplastik des Seneser Doms'. *Kunstgesch. Jahrb. der Biblioteca Hertziana* I (1937), who also discusses their condition at that time. For the dating of the sequence of the sculpture, see E. Carli, *Sculture del Duomo di Siena* (Turin, 1941) and for the documents relating to Giovanni's sojourn in Siena, see P. Bacci, 'Documenti e Commenti per la Storia dell' Arte', in *Le Arti* IV (1941–2). J. Pope-Hennessy's essay on the acquisition of the Haggai for the Victoria & Albert Museum in his *Essays on Italian Sculpture* (Phaidon, 1968) contains valuable recent information on the condition of the sculpture and both Pope-Hennessy (Phaidon, 1955) and John White (Pelican History of Art, 1966) discuss the façade in their surveys of the period.

Wood and Ivory Carvings

THE PLATES in this section illustrate individual carvings which are independent of any large complex of sculpture. They therefore do not fall in chronological order.

Only three works in wood, all crucifixes, survive from his activity in this field. None is documented and only one of them is undisputed as to its authorship. This is the painted wooden crucifix, 105 cms. in height, in the Church of S. Andrea at Pistoia (**113.** Cat. **269**), which closely resembles the Crucifixion on the marble relief of the pulpit in the same church and is assumed to have been carved at much the same time. It has been heavily re-painted; successive layers of paint have long buried the original polychrome and also obscure the subtleties of the surface of the carving. The wood would originally have received a single thin covering of gesso, upon which the colouring would have been thinly and delicately laid. The crucifix, 75 cms. in height, now in the Cathedral Museum at Siena (detail **111.** Cat. **267**), is even more heavily coated with paint than the Pistoia figure. It was first published by De Nicola as from the circle of Giovanni. Valentiner attributed it to Nicola di Nuto, Keller to an unknown Sienese. Carli, Frankovich, Pope-Hennessy and White accept it as by Giovanni. Although no documents exist to confirm or disprove these attributions, no other crucifixes of this particular type have survived and, as Pope-Hennessy says, 'this type of crucified Christ represented in the Pistoia and Siena Crucifixes is personal to Giovanni Pisano and seems not to have been imitated in other localities or by other artists.'

The third crucifix, now in the Dahlem Museum in Berlin (**112.** Cat. **268**), is a fragment and is not painted. Carved in boxwood and lacking arms, feet and cross, it may be closely compared with the Siena crucifix and is to me convincing as Giovanni's work, but it is no more wholeheartedly accepted by experts than the Siena figure. Frankovich accepts it. Keller does not. If these three works are by Giovanni they could be dated approximately as having been carved between 1290 and 1301.

The fragment of an ivory crucifix (**114, 115.** Cat. **270**) in the Victoria and Albert Museum, published by Pope-Hennessy in 1951, is also closely related in style to the Siena figure and his attribution carries complete conviction. The arguments which he advances have not, to my knowledge, been questioned and his tentative dating of the figure at 1300 squares with the probability that the fragmentary ivory crucifix is connected with the ivory Madonna and Child, first published by Supino in 1904 and now in the Museo San Matteo at Pisa (**116, 117**). The documents relating to this ivory are fairly numerous and were published by R. Barsotti. They date from a notarized contract of 1298 or 1299 (the date is disputable) between Giovanni and the Chapter of the Pisa Cathedral. Giovanni was to complete certain works by Christmas under penalty of the exceptionally heavy fine of 100 lire. This is the sole surviving document which specifically names Giovanni as a carver in this medium and the commission was obviously so important that the Madonna and Child, which is an unusually large ivory, 53 cms. in height, is assumed to have been part of it, whilst the fact that several ivories are stipulated in the contract has been taken to mean that the whole work in its original form consisted of the *tabula* with images in ivory which is noted in the cathedral inventory in 1369: *Tabulam unam eburneam ab altari majori cum ymaginibus. Ciborium unum de ligno deaurato quod super-*

ponitur in medio dicte tabule in quo est ymago Beate Marie in medio duorum Angelorum de ebore. This work was subsequently described in 1433 as a table in several sections bearing a Madonna and Child with two angels (with metal wings) holding candelabra, and two scenes of the Passion: '*I tabula in multis petiis cum tabernaculo in medio cum Virgine Maria et Filio in collo et duobus Angelis cum celostribus in manibus et cum alis ferreis. Que figure sunt erburnee et duo petia cum storia Passionis Domini Nostri Jhesu Christi. Que figure sunt erburnee et deficit una figura ab una partium.*' It stood upon the high altar of the cathedral and it is with one of the two Passion scenes from the *tabula* that Pope-Hennessy associates the ivory crucifix. Its size (13.27 cms.) would make such a formal relationship to the Madonna probable.

The history of this ivory composition and its vicissitudes is documented in the *Archivo Capitolare di Pisa.* Apart from the references mentioned, there are notes of payments made for repairs in August and September 1452; these were for gilding, staining and colouring. Following the great fire in the cathedral, there is a reference in 1595 to the fact that the work was saved and stored in a room in the *Casa dell'Opera* together with various other objects. At this date the whole table was intact save for some damage to the angels. By 1603, however, the damage had become so serious that the work was replaced in the Cathedral by a new wooden Madonna and by 1608 only the Madonna and two angels from the *tabula* could be found, in a condition which rendered them so useless that they were once again stored, this time in an attic over some workmen's bedrooms in the *Casa dell'Opera.* In August 1634 the Madonna was removed from store and in 1635 a new head and a foot were carved for the Child and a new hand for the Madonna. Her draperies were repaired and she was given a new ebony base, this work being carried out under the supervision of a certain Giovanni Battista Riminaldi. The ivory was also whitened. In 1700 an engraving of the Madonna was reproduced in *Theatrum Basilicae Pisae* by J. Martini which shows that at that time the Child held an orb in His left hand rather than His right and that His right hand was raised in a gesture of benediction. A final reference in the cathedral inventory of 1816 valued the piece at 105 lire, precisely five lire more, without allowing for a change in the value of the lira, than Giovanni would have been fined had he not completed the whole work. The date of the ivory has been disputed by Ragghianti, who places it as early as 1265 and also maintains that the Child's head, as it now appears, is nineteenth-century. The influences to be seen in the work are French and its most obvious forerunner is the statue of the Virgin on the north portal of Notre Dame. (Fig. c)

Apart from Pope-Hennessy's publication of the ivory crucifix, reprinted in his *Essays on Italian Sculpture*, which discusses the relationship of all the work illustrated in this section, the main references to the woodcarvings are G. de Nicola, 'Studi sull' arte Senese II. Di alcune sculture nel Duomo di Siena', *Rassegna d'Arte* (1918); W. R. Valentiner, 'Observations on Sienese and Pisan Trecento Sculpture', *The Art Bulletin* (1927); G. de Frankovich, 'L'Origine e la diffusione del Cristo gotico doloroso', *Jahrb. der Biblioteca Hertziana* (1938); Keller, *Giovanni Pisano;* and E. Carli, *Il Museo dell' Opera e la Libraria Piccolomini* (Siena, 1946) and *Antica Scultura Lignea Senese* (Florence, 1949). On the Ivory Madonna: J. B. Supino, *Arte Pisana* (Pisa, 1904); R. Koechlin, *Les Ivoires Gothiques Françaises* II (Paris, 1924); C. R. Ragghianti, 'La Madonna eburnea di Giovanni Pisano', *Critica d'Arte* IV (1954); and R. Barsotti, 'Nuovi studi sulla Madonna eburnea di Giovanni Pisano', *Critica d'Arte* XIX (1957) are the most important. M. Weinberger's 'Die Madonna am Nordportal von Notre Dame' in *Zeitschrift für bildende Kunst* LXIV (1930–31) is also relevant.

The Marble Madonna Groups

OF THE FIVE Madonnas illustrated, all are individual sculptures with the exception of the fragmentary *Madonna di Arrigo* (**122.** Cat. **277**), which originally formed part of a group consisting of a now lost statue of the Emperor Henry and the personification of Pisa (Cat. **278**). This group originally stood in the tympanum of the Ranieri door of Pisa Cathedral. At various times during his career, Giovanni was commissioned to carve Madonnas either for the tympana of doors or to stand, in one or possibly two surviving cases, upon the altar. The standing half-length figure, increased by an additional section from the height of 97 to 132 cms. (**118.** Cat. **272**) and now in the Pisan Campo Santo, is assumed by Keller and Weinberger to be the earliest of the tympanum figures and Giovanni's first independent work. It stood originally over the west door of the cathedral. Barsotti, however, dates the work at 1302 as the result of a recently discovered document concerning a block of marble to be used for the purpose of carving such a figure for the *maiori ecclesia* at that time. The problem is not resolved. The sculpture was discovered in 1829 among scattered marbles in the Campo Santo and first attributed to Giovanni at that time by Rosini. It was taken to the Museo San Matteo (then known as the Museo Civico) in 1935. It has since been returned to the Campo Santo, where it is now exhibited.

The Madonna for the tympanum of the principal door of the Pisa Baptistry (**119, 120.** Cat. **273**) was carved in high relief after Giovanni's return from Siena in 1297. It too now stands in the Campo Santo in a state of dilapidation and covered with dirt, between two figures of St John the Baptist and St John the Evangelist, by different sculptors. The Child has been severely damaged and His feet are missing. The head has been broken off and re-set at an unconvincing angle. The statue is in comparatively shallow relief, the depth of the block being 42 cms., hollowed out at the back to the depth of 9 cms. It stands 180 cms. in height, with a lateral measurement of 66 cms. An inscription on the base (30 × 66 cms.) reads:

SUB PETRI CURA   HAEC PIA FUIT SCULPTA FIGURA
NICOLI NATO   SCULPTORE JOHANNE VOCATO

The Madonna for the Arena (or Scrovegni) Chapel at Padua (**121.** Cat. **275**) may also have been carved for the tympanum of the door of that building, but if this was the case, it was placed upon the altar in the chapel at a date early enough to preserve it in excellent condition. It is flanked by angels which, if they are not by Giovanni, are exceptional products of his workshop (Cat. **274, 276**). The work can be securely dated between 1305 and 1306. (Dimensions: 129 × 43 × 24 cms.)

The shattered condition of the *Madonna di Arrigo* (94.75 × 53.5 × 56 cms.) (**122.** Cat. **277**) is discussed in the text. It stands today in the Campo Santo, but the companion figure of *Pisa* is not at present exhibited, as it should be, as part of the group.

The *Madonna della Cintola* (detail **123.** Cat. **279**) stands on the altar of the Chapel of the Holy Girdle on the left of the nave of Prato Cathedral. Generally considered to be Giovanni's final surviving work, executed after 1312, this small and very perfect statue, 69 cms. in height, is considered by Marcenaro on stylistic grounds to be earlier than the Madonna for the tomb of Margaret of Luxembourg. The Madonna della Cintola is undocumented and unsigned. It is of highly polished marble with gilding on the crown and mantle and is without blemish save for the halo added to the head of the Child.

The Madonnas are all discussed by Keller, *op. cit.* by White, *op. cit.*, and by Pope-Hennessy, *op. cit.* The *Madonna di Arrigo* has received particular attention and has been wrongly attributed in the past to Tino da Camaino. The principal references to this Madonna are: R. Papini, *Catalogo delle Cose d'Arte d'Antichità d'Italia* (Rome, 1914). M. Weinberger, 'Eine Madonna von Giovanni Pisano', *Jahrb. d. Preuss. Kunstsammlungen* **51** II–III (1930) and 'Giovanni Pisano; a new discovery', *Burlington* LXX (1937) (in which he published the head of the figure of the personification of Pisa for the first time); M. Marangoni, 'Sculture inedite del Campo Santo di Pisa', *L'Arte* XXV (1932); E. Carli, *Tino da Camaino, Scultore* (Florence, 1934); W. R. Valentiner, *Tino da Camaino* (Paris, 1935); C. Paccagnini, 'Note sullo stile tardo di Giovanni Pisano', *Belle Arte* I (1946–48).

The Pulpit for the Church of S. Andrea, Pistoia

THE INSCRIPTION which encircles the pulpit dates its completion as 1301 and names as donor the Canon Arnoldus. If, as Vasari states, the work took four years to complete, it would have been begun immediately after Giovanni's removal from Siena and before he signed a contract with the Pisa Cathedral authorities in December 1297. The work upon which he was engaged at Pisa during those years argues that the elements of the Pistoia pulpit were carved in his workshop at Pisa and transported for erection at Pistoia either in their final form or near completion.

Of all Giovanni's major works, the Pistoia pulpit is the most perfectly preserved, having escaped the weathering to which his external sculpture was inevitably subjected, the dismantling and reconstruction which was the fate of his Pisa Cathedral pulpit and the extensive destruction which accompanied the dismemberment of the tomb of Margaret of Luxembourg. Sheltered as the Pistoia pulpit has always been from the elements, it has also escaped political iconoclasm and

the whims of ecclesiastical fashion in church ornament. Every mark of Giovanni's chisel may still be read on the surface and the only serious deprivation which we must accept today is the possible loss of polychrome and the evident loss of the inlays of vitreous paste which enhanced the depth of the relief. Some fragments of this dark-green and red vitreous paste, bearing a gold quatrefoil pattern, still adhere to the reliefs, notably behind the figure of a servant who pours water, in the panel showing the Nativity **(134)**.

Giovanni's debt to both his father's pulpits is acknowledged at Pistoia where, despite the impression of slender and aspiring verticality which he gives to his structure, it is closer in design to the massive architecture of the Pisa Baptistry pulpit than to that of Siena. Iconographically, the Pistoia narrative relief panels are no less rich than those of Siena, but they are composed with a greater rhythmic sweep in the relationships of the figures, so that the flow and counterflow of forms is less constricted.

Whilst in several of the panels, notably the Crucifixion **(141. Cat. 240)**, Giovanni incorporates motifs from the Siena pulpit, in others his composition is wholly different. In the Nativity **(131–134)**, the Adoration of the Magi **(135)** and the Massacre of the Innocents **(140)** there is a largeness of form and an elaboration of movement among the individuals portrayed which is governed by control of the relationships of each movement to the whole, a sculptural advance of great importance. The appearance of figures stacked upon one another, which Nicola did not always avoid, is gone. In addition, Giovanni achieved a dramatic chiaroscuro which Nicola did not attempt. By deep undercutting, sometimes as deep as 17 cms., into the block (the area behind Mary's head in the Nativity is a case in point) an interplay of light in contrast to dense shadow creates a formal tension and a mystery which had not been previously seen in narrative sculpture in Italy. Pope-Hennessy has remarked that Giovanni may have been moved by French ivory carvings of the class of the Soissons Diptych where a comparable elaboration of undercutting obtains; in any case, the hollowing out of those pools of darkness, once further enhanced by the use of vitreous paste, is one of the two factors which most clearly demonstrate his development at Pistoia. The other factor at once evident at Pistoia is the developed contraposto of the figures; in this Giovanni further increased the extension of axiality which he had achieved in his monumental sculpture at Siena and Pisa. Nicola's sculpture is designed to be seen from a single frontal viewpoint. The Pistoia reliefs and in particular the figures of the sibyls demand to be viewed from oblique angles no less than from in front. The spectator, in movement round the pulpit, is given a seemingly inexhaustible series of considered, related and self-enhancing compositions from whatever angle his glance may fall. In general, Giovanni held closely to his father's iconography, though he made one notable innovation in his addition to the prophets shown in the spandrels: namely, the three seated and three standing sibyls (**144–146, 149–151**). The iconographic significance of these figures is discussed in the main text and in the relevant footnote to Chapter 7.

The Church of S. Andrea, in which the pulpit stands on the left-hand side of the central nave, is a Romanesque basilica terminating in a semicircular apse. The interior of the church is austere and the pulpit stands between two simple columns with finely carved quasi-Corinthian capitals. The pulpit (**125** and detail **126**) is 389 cms. in height and stands on a raised pavement 6.5 cms. in height. The pulpit is hexagonal and is supported on seven columns of antique marbles, three of which stand on the ground and four of which stand on carved supports; of these, the central column is supported by a group of a lion, an eagle and a griffin (**153, Cat. 263, 264**). Of the surrounding columns, one stands on a lion (80.75 × 98 × 42 cms. Cat. **266**);

another on a lioness with cubs (78 × 106 × 37.25 cms. **154. Cat. 265**) and the third on a crouched figure of Atlas (88 × 62 × 47 cms. **152. Cat. 262**). This figure, despite its Lombard and French forerunners (there are comparable figures at Strasbourg (Fig. *e*) and Reims, dating from the first half of the thirteenth century), is closer in feeling to the antique than to any medieval sculpture. The outer columns rise to acanthus capitals which support an archevolt of gothic arches and spandrels upon which the figures of the prophets are carved in high relief (**147, 148**). At the juncture of each pair of spandrels is the figure of a sibyl. Three sibyls are seated (**145–147**) while three are standing (**149–151**). They are of an average height of 62 cms. The upper section of the pulpit consists of five panels bearing narrative reliefs, 85 × 105 cms., divided by angle figures in high relief of an average height of 89 cms.

The narrative panels represent:

The Annunciation and Nativity
134. Details **131–133**. Cat. **234**

The Adoration of the Magi
135. Cat. **236**

The Massacre of the Innocents
140. Details **136–139**. Cat. **238**

The Crucifixion
Detail **141**. Cat. **240**.

The Last Judgement
143. Cat. **242**

The angle figures represent:

A Deacon
127. Cat. **233**

The Apocalyptic Christ
Detail **124**. Cat. **235**

The Prophet Jeremiah
129. Cat. **237**

An Angel with the Symbols of the Evangelists
128. Cat. **239**

The Writers of the Canonical Epistles
143. Cat. **241**

Four Angels Blowing Trumpets
130. Cat. **243**

Minor restorations were made to the pulpit in 1837 when the head of a young shepherd on the right in the panel of the Nativity, and the out-thrust arm and trumpet of one of the angels on the angle carving **(130)** were replaced. A note on the lecterns will be found on p. 227. They are missing, and may be those now in New York (Cat. **301**) and Berlin (Cat. **302**).

The Pistoia Pulpit is discussed at length by John White in his excellent chapter on Giovanni Pisano in *Art and Architecture in Italy 1250–1400* (Pelican History of Art, 1966); in a short monograph by Max Seidel, *Il Pulpito di Pistoia* (Sansoni, 1965); by Pope-Hennessy in *Italian Gothic Sculpture* (Phaidon, 1955); by Keller in *Giovanni Pisano* (Vienna, 1942); and in terms of French influence on the sculpture by Robert Dan Wallace in *L'Influence de la France gothique sur deux des précurseurs de la Renaissance Italienne: Nicola et Giovanni Pisano* (Geneva, 1953).

The Pisa Cathedral Pulpit

ORIGINALLY commissioned to replace the one by Guglielmo, now at Cagliari, Giovanni's last and largest pulpit proved, in its turn, a victim of fashion when, after or as a result of the great cathedral fire of 1595, it was dismantled. An opportunity to redesign parts of the interior of the cathedral in a manner fitting to the taste of the time was presented and taken and many pieces of the pulpit were stored in the Campo Santo. Nevertheless, a policy either of economy or of some vestigial reverence for Giovanni's sculpture caused the cathedral authorities to commission a Florentine sculptor, Chiarissimo Fancelli, to incorporate various ele-

ments of Giovanni's structure in a new pulpit at a cost of 400 lire. Accordingly, in 1627 Giovanni's lions **(177.** Detail **178.** Cat. **326, 327)** with the two pillars of porphyry they supported and four angle figures of prophets were adapted to suit Fancelli's simple design and Giovanni's spandrels were cunningly contrived to ornament the stairway. In 1689 the Evangelists from Giovanni's pulpit were made into the base of a Holy Water stoup and placed in the Ranieri chapel, and the general utilization of other parts throughout the cathedral continued through much of the nineteenth century. This 'barbarous dispersal', as Bacci called it, slowed down towards the latter part of that century and in 1872 a project for reassembling the pulpit was commissioned by the Commune of Pisa; the resulting *modello*, which had been placed in the Pisa Museum, was rightly and roundly attacked by Supino in 1892. It was not until 1926 that the present reconstruction was completed by Pèleo Bacci, who correlated the surviving documents for the purpose. By this time, however, some sections of the pulpit had been lost and some were dispersed abroad. Of these, two figures of sibyls were destroyed in Berlin at the end of the second world war.

Studious as Bacci's reconstruction is, it has not gone unquestioned. The orientation of the pulpit in the cathedral is wholly changed and there is reason to suppose that the ordering of the parts does not accord either visually or schematically with the sculptor's intentions, with the result that the programme of the pulpit would no longer be fully comprehensible even to a theologian of Giovanni's time. Quite apart from their theological and intellectual relationship, which would have been of primary importance in the fourteenth century, the sculptural intricacy of the monument, which was the most elaborate Giovanni made, sustains a dreadful loss if the parts are not properly related. The general unease which the great pulpit has aroused among students of the work, as com-

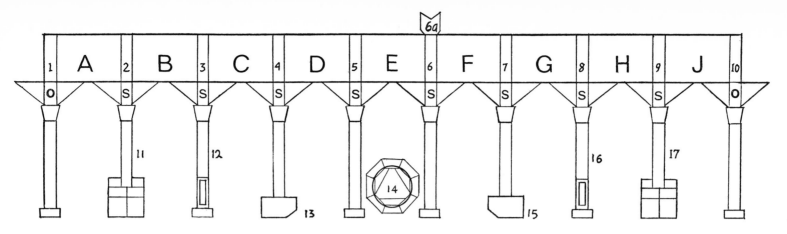

THE PISA PULPIT. *Present arrangement in Bacci's reconstruction of 1926. 1, 10. Ornaments of later date, 2. Isaiah, 3. The Apocalyptic Christ, 4. David, 5. Jeremiah, 6. Prophet (modern), 7. Malachi, 8. The Writers of the Canonical Epistles, 9. Christ in Judgement, 11. Ecclesia with figures of Prudence, Fortitude, Temperance and Justice, 12. Hercules or Samson, 13. Lion with stag, 14. The Liberal Arts and Theological Virtues, 15. Lion* with horse, *16. St Michael, 17. Christ with the Four Evangelists and figures of Giovanni Pisano and Nello di Falcone (?). A. The Birth of John the Baptist, B. The Birth of Christ, C. The Adoration of the Magi, D. The Presentation and Flight into Egypt, E. The Massacre of the Innocents, F. The Passion, G. The Crucifixion, H. J. The Last Judgement, S. Sibyls, 6 a. Gospel lectern in the form of an eagle*

pared to the felicitous pulpit at Pistoia, augmented as it is by Giovanni's own 'confession' in his inscription (which, it seems, originally ran beneath the narrative panels and not round the base) may well be, in part, the result of the disorientation of the whole and of the parts as the pulpit now stands.

A diagram made in 1595 by Adriano dell' Osta, and here adapted, shows the present and the original location of the pulpit in relation to the choir. It has been argued by Jászai that this orientation was of great programmatic importance in terms of its 'message'. According to Jászai, two lecterns originally placed opposite one another (Cat. **300, 301 a**) represented the Gospels (an eagle) and the Epistles (the Corpus Christi) and the whole relationship of the panels and the supports to these sources of discourse was determined by that division, whilst the sculptural elements which faced the nave and the congregation related to this fact as did those elements which faced the clergy in the choir. If Jászai is correct we are now presented with a relatively meaningless relationship of the parts. In any case, with the pulpit in its present position, we are given *an unintended play of light* on the monument which must negate the sculptor's conception. The importance of the intended fall of light upon a relief carving cannot be overemphasized, and I write as a working sculptor in this field. Whatever the distinction in the quality of the carving of the parts and the evidence of Giovanni's own hand in that carving, his use of chiaroscuro and the extent, in his reliefs, to which he created figures so deeply

cut as to be almost in the round is advanced even further at Pisa than it had been at Pistoia, whilst the skill with which he had learned to lead the eye across the narratives in surging rhythms, broken by abrupt descents into darkness, has never been surpassed. The fall of light was, but no longer is, an absolutely essential factor in the success of such a conception, for it is balanced on a knife edge between sculptural and pictorial vision. It is the very fact that Giovanni extended the possibility to its ultimate limits that left him unsurpassed and inimitable. The future of such conceptual illusion lay in the hands of the painters.

The symbolic association of the parts of the pulpit with one another is of such a complexity that I cannot pretend to the knowledge, nor is there space here, to elaborate upon them. By an exercise of the imagination it is possible to conceive the absolute command Giovanni must have exercised in carrying the spectator's eye, no less than his mind, through the meaningful intricacies of the monument. The most extraordinary development, which may be guessed at in contemplating the pulpit, even in its present place and form, is the extent to which the separate sculptures were made to relate to one another, not only frontally but laterally, vertically and diagonally. At Pistoia, the spectator was no longer faced, in the narrative panels, with a stone lantern lecture in which frontality dominated. At Pisa, the curved panels further contribute to a matchless cohesion of formal elements metaphorically as compact and as integral to one another as

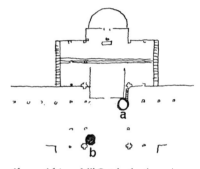

Above: Adriano dell'Osta's plan (1595) adapted to show the reorientation of Giovanni Pisano's pulpit: a. original position; b. present position. Below: pulpit by Chiarissimo Fancelli constructed in 1627, incorporating parts of Giovanni Pisano's original

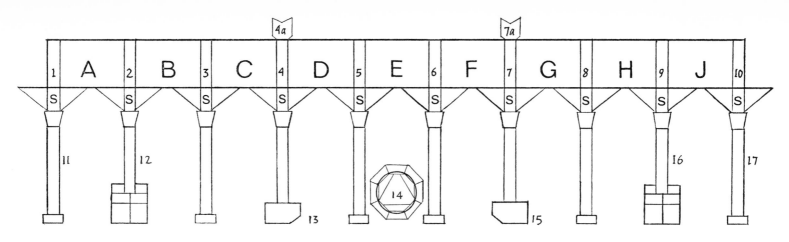

THE PISA PULPIT. *Suggested reconstruction by G. Jászai.* *(Elevation and ground plan) 1. Isaiah, 2. David, 3. Ezekiel (?), 4. Angel with symbols of the Evangelists (Metropolitan Museum, New York), 4a. Eagle Lectern, 5. John the Baptist (?), 6. The Apocalyptic Christ, 7. The Writers of the Canonical* *Epistles, 7a. Corpus Christi lectern, 8, 10. Angels (Metropolitan Museum, New York), 9. Christ in Judgement, 11. Samson, 12. Ecclesia etc., 13. Lion with stag, 14. Liberal Arts, etc., 15. Lion with horse, 16. Christ, etc., 17. St Michael. The Panels (A–J) are the same as on Bacci's reconstruction.*

the components of the human brain, whilst the supporting sculptures are no longer decorative architectural addenda but act as channels comparable to the blood vessels which carry blood to the brain from the heart. This stone anatomy cannot be adequately shown in the plates of a book, which can illustrate no more than details, drawing especial attention to those aspects of the whole which seem to show the greatest evidence of Giovanni's own hand.

Perhaps the most personal testament of all is the possible self-portrait, but even this cannot be securely identified. On each of two of the faces of the block from which the four Evangelists are carved is a relief of a man in early fourteenth-century costume. One represents a figure kneeling in the traditional pose of a donor (**171.** Cat. **317**), the other, who crouches between St Mark and St Matthew, is a smaller figure in the attitude of an Atlas (**155**). One of these figures may represent Giovanni himself and the other may represent Nello di Falcone, but neither seems likely to show Burgundio di Tado, in view of the quarrel which is presumed to have taken place, and Burgundio's separate inscription (see Ch. 8). If Giovanni has shown himself in one of these reliefs, it seems to me probable that he is the smaller figure, which is not in the conventional pose of a donor. Furthermore, the small figure has a relation to the monument which seems deliberately to indicate a physical participation in the work.

It cannot be over emphasized that those parts of the whole work which were carved by Giovanni

himself, as opposed to those by his assistants, can, at present, only be assessed by stylistic comparison, quality and other subjective standards of judgment. Weinberger is convincing when he assigns the surviving sibyls to an inferior hand, with the exception perhaps of the two destroyed in Berlin (**167.** Cat. **303, 304**). For my part, I find the Evangelists (Cat. **316**), the panel of the Annunciation, Visitation and Birth of the Baptist (**156.** Cat. **281**), the Liberal Arts (**168.** Cat. **321–325**), the Hercules or Samson (**170.** Cat. **311**), the Virtues (details **172, 173.** Cat. **313, 314**), the Ecclesia (detail **174.** Cat. **312**), and the Lions (**177** and detail **178.** Cat. **326, 327**) all speak to me in Giovanni's unique voice and I agree with White that the magnificent detail of the base of the panel showing the Elect at the Last Judgement (**165**) is an epitome of that high drama which only he could have carved. White goes on to make the valid point that whatever weakness in detail may be discerned in several of the panels, especially that of the Passion, the design of the narratives with their astonishing wealth of invention represents a culmination of the steady increase in descriptive naturalism which joins all four pulpits by Nicola and Giovanni. In this, no less than in the field of monumental sculpture, Giovanni must be reckoned one of the greatest innovators in the history of his art.

The Pisa Cathedral pulpit is not only far more elaborate than that at Pistoia, consisting as it does of an octagon with two additional entrance panels in the form of an ambo, but it is very considerably larger. Compared to the Pistoia pulpit, which is 389 cms. in height, the Pisa pulpit is 433 cms.; also the structure at Pisa is volumetrically much larger, being conceived in massively horizontal terms as opposed to the verticality of the pulpit at Pistoia. At Pisa, the supports are now eleven in number, as opposed to seven at Pistoia, but may originally have been thirteen. They now consist of four plain columns of antique marbles, two of porphyry and two of brocatello; two shorter porphyry columns supported by lions, one of which (87.5 ×122 × 43.5 cms.) grapples a dying horse **(177)** and one (88.5 × 125.75 × 51 cms.) a dead deer (detail **178).** Of the remaining carved supports, two consist of single figures in the round standing on decorated rectangular plinths. These are a figure of St Michael, which has been attributed to Tino da Camaino **(169. Cat. 310),** 106 cms. in height, and a Hercules or Samson **(170. Cat. 311),** 103.5 cms. in height. Two further outer supports consist of groups, one of which shows the Four Evangelists (detail **155. Cat. 316),** and the two 'portraits' carved from a block. This group measures 122 × 90 × 47 cms. and supports the figure of Christ (detail **176. Cat. 315),** 119 cms. in height. The second sculptural group shows the Four Cardinal Virtues (details **172, 173. Cat. 313, 314)** carved from a block 123 × 89 × 51 cms. in size which supports the figure of Ecclesia, 126 cms. in height, while the central support of the pulpit rises from an octagonal base 39 cms. high with faces 25 cms. in width, upon which are carved the Eight Liberal Arts. Above the Liberal Arts stand three caryatids representing the Theological Virtues, which vary in height between 157.5 and 162 cms. **(175. Cat. 318–320).**

The capitals of the columns and the supports are antique, with the exception of two copied from the Pistoia pulpit. The narrative panels represent:

The Annunciation, Visitation and Birth of the Baptist
156. Cat. 281
85 ×107 cms.

The Nativity
162. Cat. 283
83 ×107 cms.

The Arrival, Adoration and Dream of the Magi
Cat. **285**
83 × 112 cms.

The Presentation in the Temple and the Flight into Egypt
Detail **163. Cat. 288**
83 × 111.75 cms.

The Massacre of the Innocents
Detail **165. Cat. 290**
83 × 112.5 cms.

The Passion of Christ
Cat. **291**
83 × 112 cms.

The Crucifixion
164. Cat. 293
83 × 112.5 cms.

The Elect at the Judgement
165. Cat. 297
83 × 112.5 cms.

The Damned at the Judgement
Cat. **299**
85 × 110.5 cms.

With the exception of the panel of the Birth of the Baptist and that of the Damned, which are flat, the panels are all curved. The depth of undercut of the relief is so great in several places that at midday the stone may be seen to be translucent. In the Massacre of the Innocents, for instance, and in the Elect, the marble is in parts excavated to a depth of 18 cms. in the 22-cms. slab.

Between the narrative panels, as the pulpit is now, stand angle statues of four prophets bearing scrolls. They are identified by Bacci as Isaiah **(157.**

Cat. **282),** David **(159.** Cat. **286),** Jeremiah **(160.** Cat. **289)** and Malachi **(161.** Cat. **292).** In addition to these are representations of the Writers of the Canonical Epistles (Cat. **294),** the Apocalyptic Christ **(158.** Cat. **284)** and Christ in Judgement **(166.** Cat. **298).** There is also a copy of an unidentified prophet, which Keller maintains replaces a lost group of Evangelists. Jászai, in rearranging the sequence, rejects the identification of Jeremiah and Malachi, re-naming them Ezekiel and John the Baptist. He also increases the number of angle statues from eight to ten by including the Symbols of the Evangelists (Cat. **287)** and the two groups of angels playing trumpets (Cat. **295, 296)** which are now in the Metropolitan Museum, New York. This he does by discarding the copy of the prophet and proposing the angel groups to have occupied the place of the two panels of ornament which at present terminate the quasi-ambo. In making this putative reconstruction he also restores to the original conception the sum of ten sibyls, which would accord with the traditional number stipulated by Lactantius. Of the eight sibyls which at present occupy the areas between the foliate arched spandrels below the narrative panels, three are modern, two replacing the now destroyed figures previously in Berlin. The head and communicating angel of a fourth is also modern whilst four (Cat. **306–309)** are probably contemporary with the structure, but the work of an assistant to Giovanni, as indeed, as Weinberger suggests, are the spandrel figures themselves. The height of the spandrels is 58 cms., the prophets contained in them 33 cms. and the sibyls an average of 55.5 cms.

The pulpit is surmounted by an eagle lectern for the Gospel reading (Cat. **300)** and was also surmounted, according to Jászoa, by another for the reading of the Epistles. He suggests that this was the fragment still embedded in the wall of the cathedral (Cat. **301a).** Two other lecterns, an eagle (Cat. **301,** now in the Metropolitan Museum) and a 'Corpus Christi' lectern (Cat. **302,** Berlin

Dahlem) which have been associated with Pisa are thought by Jászai to have belonged to the Pistoia pulpit.

The damage and the restorations otherwise sustained by the pulpit consist, in the supports, of the lion on the shoulders of Hercules (or Samson) and the cherubim above the shoulders of Christ. The head of an angel in the Nativity Panel and various architectural elements are also restored.

The formidable body of scholarly deliberation on the Pisa pulpit and its reconstruction will be found in the general bibliography. The works most relevant to these Plate Notes are: P. Bacci, *La Ricostruzione del Pergamo di Giovanni Pisano nel Duomo di Pisa* (Milan and Rome, 1926). This contains the documents; R. Papini, 'Pro Memoria sull' classicità di Giovanni Pisano', in *Miscellania in onore di J. B. Supino* (Florence, 1933), with particular reference to the classical sources of the reliefs; M. Weinberger, 'Remarks on the techniques of the master's workshop', *Burlington Magazine* LXX (1937); H. Keller, *Giovanni Pisano;* G. Jászai, *Die Pisaner Domkanzel* (Munich, 1968); also the chapter on the subject by John White in *Art and Architecture in Italy 1250–1400.*

The Tomb of Margaret of Luxembourg

THIS TOMB, the last major work by Giovanni Pisano known to us, was begun soon after December 1311 when the Countess Margaret, born Margaret of Brabant, wife of the then uncrowned Emperor Henry VII, died of the plague at Genoa. She was buried there, in the church of S. Francesco di Casteletto, and Giovanni was appointed 'Sculptor of the Queen's Sepulchre' by the Emperor.

The sections of the tomb, which was of Carrara marble, are likely to have been carved in Giovanni's workshop at Pisa, but he was in Genoa in August 1312, presumably to supervise the erection of the monument, and there received a payment of 81 gold florins, at the command of the Emperor, from the archdeacon of the church.

S. Francesco di Casteletto and the tomb were demolished in 1798. In 1874 the largest surviving fragment, a group representing Margaret being raised from the dead by two angels **(180–183.** Cat. **328),** was removed from the Villa Brignole Sale at Voltri and is now in the Museum of the Palazzo Bianco in Genoa.

In 1960 a figure of Justice **(184–186).** Cat. **329),** who bears a small scroll carved with the words *Dilecisti justitiam odisti iniquitatem,* was discovered near Genoa by Dr Caterina Marcenaro, who identified it as one of the four figures of Virtues which she believed had originally formed part of the tomb. This attribution was supported by Torreti and the deduction was aided by the existence of a group of Virtues by an undistinguished mid-fourteenth-century sculptor, perhaps associated with the circle of Giovanni di Balduccio, which now stands on a balustrade above the vestibule of the Genoese church of S. Maria Maddalena. The figure of Justice from this group, so clearly inferior and yet sufficiently close in pose and in her attributes to the newly discovered carving, argued an unskilful artisan who had taken his motif from a great sculptor. Furthermore, its modest size and the proportions of the Justice to the fragments of Margaret and the angels were sufficiently related to have been part of the same monument. The Justice passed briefly on to the art market, but was acquired by the Italian State and is now in the Palazzo Rosso in Genoa.

In 1962, Dr Marcenaro also established the connection between a Madonna **(187, 188.** Cat. **330)** which had long stood in the Genoa Museum of S. Agostino, and the tomb of Margaret. The history of this figure, in the museum records, consisted solely of the information that it had come, at a date un-specified, from Sampierdarano. In 1939 it was recognized by Valentiner and moved from obscurity to a place abutting Margaret and the angels, then in the same museum, but the Madonna was not identified with the tomb at that date. Valentiner did not publish it and it was not even thought to be of sufficient interest to be evacuated as a precaution in wartime. When Dr Marcenaro rediscovered it in 1960 it stood on a parapet of the convent next to S. Agostino amidst an indescribable confusion of unclassified marbles. It is to be hoped that the Justice and the Madonna will presently join Margaret and the angels in the Palazzo Bianco.

One further fragment of the tomb, the head of Temperance **(189.** Cat. **331),** was acquired by a private collector in Switzerland in 1942. The relative proportions of these fragments go far to confirm the fact that they all once formed part of the same sculptural complex. The fragment of Margaret and the angels measures 73.5 × 64 × 30.5 cms. The angels measure 68.3 × 30.5 × 33.5 cms. and 78 × 29.7 × 33.8 cms., the headless Madonna measures 47.5 × 20 × 18 cms. and the Justice measures 98.5 × 22.75 × 30 cms. Assuming the Madonna to have been at the apex of the tomb, her modest size would have contributed to the impression of monumentality the whole tomb must have conveyed. The head of Temperance is 15.5 cms. in height and that of Justice, including her crown, is 18.5 cms. All the fragments are of Carrara marble.

The main publications connected with the newly discovered fragments of the tomb are: P. Torreti, 'Una Statua della Giustizia di Giovanni Pisano per il Monumento di Margherita di Brabante in Genova', *Commentari* III–IV (1960); C. Marcenaro, 'Per la Tomba di Margherita di Brabante', *Paragone* 167 (1963); M. Seidel, 'Ein neu entdecktes Fragment des Genoveser Grabmals der Königin Margarethe von Giovanni Pisano', *Pantheon* XXXVI, 5 (Sept.-Oct. 1968).

Catalogue Raisonné of the Works of Giovanni Pisano

Numbers in brackets refer to the plates in the body of the book.
Works shown in detail in the plates are reproduced complete in the catalogue.

190   191   192   193

194   195   196   197

198   199   200   201   202

203

204

205

206

207

208

209

210

211

212

213

214

215

216

217

218

219

220 221 222 223 224 225

226

227

228

229

230

231

232

233

234

235

236

237

238

239

240

241

242   243   244   245

246   247   248   249

250   251   252   253

254

255

256

257

258

259

260

261

262

263

264

265

266

267

268

269

270

271

272

273

274

275

276

277

278

279

280

281

282

283

284

285

286

287

288

289

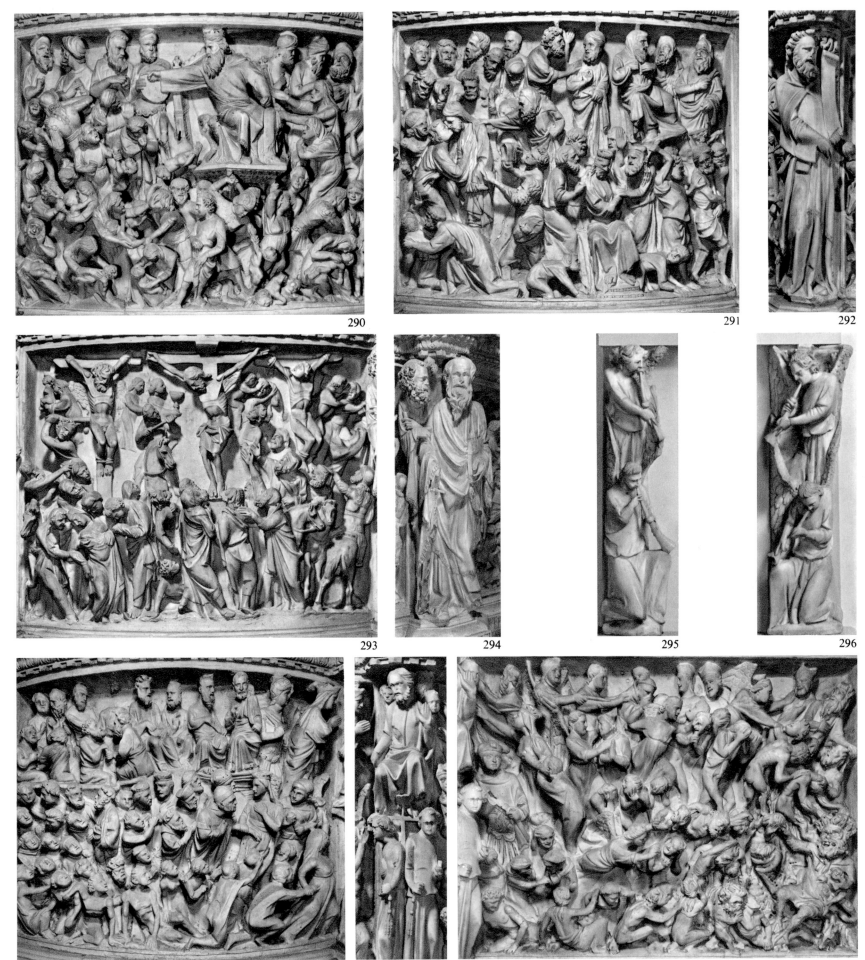

290

291

292

293

294

295

296

297

298

299

300

301

301a

302

303

304

305

306

307

308

309

310

311

312

313

314

315

316

317

318   319

320

321

322   323

324

325

326   327

328

329

330

331

332

338

333

339

334

340

335

341

336

342

343

337

344

The Gradule

SHORTLY before beginning work on the Pisa pulpit, Giovanni was responsible for the *gradule* or stair rises for the steps leading up to the main door of the Cathedral. How much of the work is from his own hand is conjectural. An inscription which does not mention Giovanni by name records the construction as follows:

IN NOMINE DNI AMEN. BORGHOGNO DI TADO OPERAJO DELL'OPERA DI SCA MARIA FECE FARE TUTTI QUESTI GRADI LI QUAL SONO INTORNO QUESTA ECOLIA DELLO DUOMO ET FUNO INCHOMINCIATA ANN DNI CUR MCCLXXXXVII FURO FINITI ANI DNI MCCC

(In the name of the Lord, Amen. Burgundio di Tado clerk of the works of Santa Maria had made all these steps which are around the cathedral causing them to be begun in 1297 and finished in 1300)

Each of the small reliefs is framed in a rectangle in the long length of the stone. All are severely worn and the birds especially are nearly indecipherable. The *gradule* are now in the Museo San Matteo and are shown in fifteen varying lengths. They are described in the sequence in which they are displayed in the museum:

Two bearded heads and two heads of ram and eagle
Unillustrated
29.5 × 130.9 cms.

Three birds (water fowl)
Cat. 332
30 × 94.5 cms.

Three heads of putti, the centre one with a winged headdress
Cat. 333
30 × 107.5 cms.

A ram, a sheep, a ram and a calf
Cat. 334
29.25 × 157 cms.

Four male heads, three bearded, one crowned
Cat. 335
31 × 145 cms.

Heads of a monkey, a lion and a calf
Cat. 336
30 × 100 cms.

A dog, a lion and a dog
Cat. 337
30 × 103.5 cms.

Heads of a calf, a mule, a boar and a bear
Cat. 338
30 × 102 cms.

A lion's head and three human heads, full and three-quarter face
Cat. 339
30 × 137.75 cms.

Six male heads, four bearded, all facing right and gazing upwards
Cat. 340
30 × 210 cms.

Six male heads, in pairs, facing inwards
Unillustrated
30 × 233 cms.

Six male heads, in pairs, facing inwards, two in pointed hoods
Cat. 341
30 × 213 cms.

Three tonsured male heads, a helmeted head, the heads of a horse, a bull and two donkeys
Cat. 342
30 × 266 cms.

Six male heads facing inwards in pairs (mythical figures?)
Cat. 343
30 × 229 cms.

Seven bearded male heads, six in pairs facing inwards
Cat. 344
30 × 246.25 cms.

The *gradule* are discussed with special relevance to the relationship between a dog (Cat. 377) and Giovanni's Wolf for Siena by E. Carli in *La Scultura del Duomo di Siena* (Turin, 1941), p. 18, figs. 12–16.

BIBLIOGRAPHY *Certain works referred to at length in the notes, both to text and plates, are not listed again here.*

ANCONA, P. D': 'Le representazioni allegoriche delle Arti Liberali nel medio evo e nel rinascimento', *Arte* 5 (1902), 211*ff.*

BACCI, P.: *Il camposanto di Pisa non e di Giovanni di Niccolo Pisano* (Pisa, 1918)
La ricostruzione del Pergamo di Giovanni Pisano nel Duomo di Pisa (Milan and Rome, 1926)
Documenti e commenti per la storia dell'arte (Florence, 1944)

BALDINUCCI, F.: 'Giovanni Pisano scultore e architetto', *Notizie* I, 97 (1767) and I, 71 (1768)

BARSOTTI, D.: 'La Madonna eburnea di Giovanni Pisano', *Critica d'Arte* 19 (1957)
'Nuova Studi sulla Madonna eburnea di Giovanni Pisano', *Critica d'Arte* 19 (1957)

BECHERUCCI, L.: 'An exhibition of Pisan Trecento sculpture', *Bulrington Magazine* 89 (1947), 68*ff.*

BERTAUX, E.: *L'Art dans l'Italie méridionale* (Paris, 1904)
'La sculpture du XIVe siècle en Italie et en Espagne', *Histoire de l'Art* II. 2, Ch. 7 (Paris, 1906)

BERTI, L.: 'Maniera di Giovanni Pisano', *Bolletino d'Arte* 37 (1952), 260*f.*

BIAGI, V.: *Per la ricostruzione del Pergamo di Giovanni Pisano* (Pisa, 1926)

BIANCHI, L.: 'La fontana di Perugia e il suo architetto', *Atti de V. Convegno Naz. di Storia dell' Architettura, Perugia 1948* (Florence, 1957), 505*ff.*

BIEHL, W. R.: *Die toskanische Plastik des frühen und hohen Mittelalters* (Leipzig, 1926)

BODE, W. VON: *Die italienische Plastik* (Berlin, 1893)

BODMER, H.: 'The reconstruction of Giovanni Pisano's pulpit in the Cathedral of Pisa', *Art in America* 15 (1926), 3*ff.*
'Die skulpierten romanischen Kanzeln in der Toskana', *Belvedere* 12 (1928) 3*ff.*

BORCHARDT, R.: 'Pisa und seine Landschaft', *Atlantis* 6 (1934), 28*ff.*
Pisa. Ein Versuch (Frankfurt a/M, 1948)
'Die Freiplastik des Giovanni Pisano', *Das Kunstwerk* VI (1952), 32

BRACH, A.: *Nicola und Giovanni Pisano und die Plastik des XIII. Jahrhunderts in Siena* (Strassburg, 1904)

BRAUNFELS, W.: 'Zur Gestalt-Ikonographie der Kanzeln des Nicola und Giovanni Pisano', *Das Münster* II (1948–49), 321*ff.*
Mittelalterliche Stadtbaukunst in der Toskana (Berlin, 1953)

BUSH-BRAUN, A.: 'Giotto: two problems in the origins of his style', *Bull.* 34 (1952), 42*ff.*

CARLI, E.: 'Per lo stile tardo di Giovanni Pisano', *Arte* 39 (1936)
Sculture del Duomo di Siena (Turin, 1941)
Il Pulpito di Siena (Bergamo, 1943)
'Per un "maestro dei Tabernacoli"', *Belle Arti* I, 2 (1946–47), 102*ff.*
Il Museo dell'Opera e la Libraria Piccolomini (Siena, 1946)
'La mostra della antica scultura pisana a Pisa', *Emporium* 105 (1947)
'Il nuovo Museo Nazionale di Pisa', *Emporium* 111 (1950), 99*ff.*
'Chefs-d'Œuvre de la sculpture du moyen-âge', *Amour de l'Art* 46–48 (1950), 35*ff.*
Nicola Pisano (Milan and Florence, 1953)
'Giovanni Pisano a Siena', *Acts of 20th International Congress of the History of Art: Romanesque and Gothic* (Princeton, 1963)
Tino da Camaino: Sculture (Florence, 1934)

La scultura lignea senese (Milan, 1954)
La scultura lignea italiana dal XII. al XVI. secolo (Paris, 1963)

CELLINI, P.: 'La "facciato semplice" del Duomo di Siena', *Proporzioni* II (1948), 55*ff.*
'Della fontana maggiore di Perugia', *Paragone* 15 (1951), 17*ff.*

CICOGNARA, L.: *Storia della scultura* (Prato, 1823–24)

COLASANTI, A.: *L'arte bizantina in Italia* (Milan, 1913)

CONTUCCI, P.: *Sculture di Giovanni da Pisa nel pergamo della chiesa di San Andrea in Pistoia* (Pistoia, 1843)

CRICHTON, G. H. & E. R.: *Nicola Pisano and the Revival of Sculpture in Italy* (Cambridge, 1938)

CROWE, SIR J. A., and G. B. CAVALCASELLE: *History of Painting in Italy*, Vol. I (London, 1864)

DAMI, L.: 'Legni policromi di Siena', *Dedalo* (1922)

DAVIDSOHN, R.: 'Giovanni Pisano in Siena im Jahre 1314', *Repertorium für Kunstwissenschaft* XXX (1907), 103*f.*

DOBBERT, E.: *Über den Styl Niccolo Pisanos und dessen Ursprung* (Munich, 1873)
'Die Pisani', in *Kunst und Künstler des Mittelalters und der Neuzeit* (Leipzig, 1877)

DVORAK, M.: *Kunstgeschichte als Geistesgeschichte* (Munich, 1924)
Geschichte der italienischen Kunst im Zeitalter der Renaissance, vols. 1–2 (Munich, 1927)

EINEM, H. VON: *Das Stutzengeschoß der Pisaner Domkanzel: Gedanken zum Alterswerk des Giovanni Pisano* (Cologne-Opladen, 1962)

EVANS, JOAN: *Art in Mediaeval France* (Oxford, 1948)

FASOLA, G. NICCO-: 'La fontana di Arnolfo', *Commentarii* II (1951), 98*ff.*

'Gli inizi della Fontana di Perugia', *Studi medievali* XVII (1951), 124*ff.*
La fontana di Perugia (Rome, 1951)
Nicola Pisano (Rome, 1941)

FIOCCO, G.: 'Giotto e Arnolfo', *Revista d'Arte* (1937), 221*ff.*

FOCILLON, HENRI: *The Art of the West:* Vol. II, *Gothic Art in the Middle Ages* (London, 1963)

FOVILLE, J. DE: *Pise et Lucques* (Paris, n. d.)

FORSTER, E.: *Geschichte der italienischen Kunst* (Leipzig, 1869)

FRANCOVICH, G. DE: 'L'origine e la diffusione del Crocifisso gotico doloroso', *Kunstgesch. Jahrbuch d. Bibl. Hertziana* II (1938)
'Studi recenti sulla scultura gotica toscana Giovanni Pisano', *Le Arti* 4 (1941–42), 195*ff.*

FRANKL, PAUL: *The Gothic: Literary Sources and Interpretation through Eight Centuries* (Princeton, 1960)

FREUD, SIGMUND: 'The Moses of Michelangelo', *Int. Psych. Library* No. 10, Vol. IV, pp. 257–287. Originally published anonymously in *Imago* III (1914)

FREUND, L.: *Studien zur Bildgeschichte der Sibyllen in der neueren Kunst.* Thesis (Hamburg, 1936)

FREY, D.: *Gotik und Renaissance* (Augsburg, 1929)

FRIED, F.: 'Zwei Engelgruppen von Giovannis Domkanzel in Pisa', *J. Strzygowski-Festschrift* (Klagenfurt, 1932), 54*ff.*

FRY, R. A.: 'A reconstructed Annunciation (Giovanni Pisano)', *The Burlington Magazine* XL (1922), 54

GASS, K. E.: *Pisaner Tagebuch* (Heidelberg-Darmstadt, 1961)

GNUDI, G.: *Nicola, Arnolfo, Lapo* (Florence, 1948)

GOLZIO, V.: 'Le Ducento et le Trecento', *L'Amour de l'Art* (1935), 151*ff.*

GRAVENKAMP, C.: 'Die Antike in der gotischen Statuarik des 13. Jahrhunderts', *Die Kunst* 81 (1939–40), 121*ff.*

HÉLIN, M.: 'Un texte inédit sur l'iconographie des sibylles', *Revue belge de philologie et d'histoire* 15 (1936), 349*ff.*

HERLIHY, D.: *Pisa in the Early Renaissance.* New Haven Misc. (Yale, 1958)
Medieval and Renaissance Pistoia. New Haven Misc. (Yale, 1967)

HOFFMANN-CURTIUS, KATHRIN: *Das Programm der Fontana Maggiore in Perugia* (Düsseldorf, 1968)

JANTZEN, H.: 'Giotto und der gotische Stil', in *Über den gotischen Kirchenraum und andere Aufsätze* (Berlin, 1951), 35*ff.*
High Gothic (New York, 1957)

JÁSZAI, GÉZA: *Die Pisaner Domkanzel.* (Thesis; Munich, 1968)

JORDAN, E.: *Les Origines de la domination angevine en Italie* (New York, 1960)

JULIAN, R.: *L'Eveil de la sculpture italienne* (Paris, 1945)

JUSTI, L.: 'Giovanni Pisano und die toskanischen Skulpturen des XIV Jahrhunderts im Berliner Museum', *Jahrbuch der Kgl. Preuss. Kunstsammlungen* 24 (1903), 247*ff.*
'Giovanni Pisano', *Im Dienste der Kunst* (Breslau, 1936) 37*ff.*

KELLER, H.: 'Die Bauplastik des Sieneser Domes. Studien zu Giovanni Pisano und seiner künstlerischen Nachfolge', *Kunstgesch. Jahrbuch d. Bibl. Hertziana* I (1937), 139*ff.*
Giovanni Pisano (Vienna, 1942)
'Neues aus der Toskana', *Kunstchronik* VI (1953), 1*ff.*

KLOTZ, H.: 'Ein Bildwerk aus der Hütte des Giovanni Pisano', *Jahrbuch der Berliner Museen* 7 (1965), 2

KOECHLIN, RAYMOND: *Les Ivoires gothiques français* (Paris, 1924)

KOVACH, F. J.: *Die Ästhetik des Thomas von Aquin. Eine genetische und systematische Analyse* (Berlin, 1961)

KRÖNIG, W.: 'Toskana und Apulien. Beiträge zum Problemkreis der Herkunft des Nicola Pisano', *Zschr. f. Kg.* 16 (1953), 101*ff.*

LAVAGNINO, E.: *Storia dell'arte medioevale italiana* (Turin, 1936)

LELARGE-DESAR, P.: 'Notes et documents: Giovanni Pisano et la cathedrale de Pise', *Revue de l'art ancien et moderne* XXXII (1912), 463*ff.*

LUSINI, V.: *Il Duomo di Siena* (Siena, 1911)

MÂLE, EMILE: *L'Art réligieuse du XIIIe siècle en France* (Paris, 1948)
Le Fin du moyen-âge en France (Paris, 1949)

MARANGONI, M.: 'Giovanni Pisano e Tino di Camaino', *Arti* 4 (1941–42), 351*ff.*
Omaggio a Giovanni Pisano (Urbino, 1943)
'Sculture inedite del Battistero Pisano', *L'Arte* (1931)
'Sculture inedite del Camposanto di Pisa', *L'Arte* XXV (1932)

MARCENARO, C.: 'Per la tomba di Margherita di Brabante', *Paragone* 133 (1961)
'La Madonna della tomba di Margherita di Brabante', *Paragone* 167 (1963)

MARLE, H. VON: 'L'Annonciation dans la sculpture monumentale de Pise et de Sienne', *Revue de l'art* I (1934), I, 111*ff.* and (1935), I, 88*ff.*

MARTINDALE, A.: review of John White, *Art and Architecture in Italy 1230–1400* in *Burlington Magazine* (Sept. 1967)

MESSERER, W.: *Das Relief im Mittelalter* (Berlin, 1959), 105*ff.*
'Einige Darstellungsprinzipien der Kunst im Mittelalter', *Dt. Vierteljahresschrift f. Lit.wiss. und Geistesgesch.* (1962)

MILANESI, G.: *Documenti per la storia dell'arte senese* (Siena, 1854)
(ed.) *Vasari. Le vite* (Siena, 1878)

MORRONA, A. DA: *Pisa illustrata nelle arti del disegno* (Leghorn, 1812)

NICCO, G.: 'Accenti del gotico', *Arte* 32 (1929), 239*ff.*

NICCOLAI, A.: *Per la ricostruzione del Pergamo di Giovanni Pisano* (Pisa, 1926)

NICOLA, G. DE: 'Studi sull'arte senese II: di alcune sculture nel Duomo di Siena', *Rassegna d'Arte* (1918)

PACCAGNINI, G.: 'Note sullo stile tardo di Giovanni Pisano', *Belle Arti* I (1946–47), 246*ff.*

PANOFSKY, E.: *Renaissance and Renascences in Western Art* (Stockholm, 1960)

PAPINI, R.: 'La collezione di sculture del Campo Santo di Pisa', *Bolletino d'Arte* 9 (1915), 169*f.*
'Pro-memoria sulla classicità di Giovanni Pisano', *Miscellanea di storia dell'arte in onore di J.B. Supino* (Florence, 1933), 113*ff.*
Catalogo delle cose d'arte d'antichità d'Italia (Rome, 1914)

PECCHIAIA, P.: *Miscellanea di erudizione* I (Pisa, 1905)

PINCHERLE, A.: *Gli Oracoli Sibillini giudaici* (Rome, 1922)

POPE-HENNESSY, JOHN: *Italian Gothic Sculpture* (London, 1955)
'Giovanni Pisano', in *Enciclopedia universale dell'Arte* (Venice and Rome, 1958), IV, 239–46
Essays on Italian Sculpture (London, 1968)

POPP, A. E.: *Niccolo and Giovanni Pisano* (1922)

PROCACCI, U.: 'Ignote sculture lignee nel Pisano', *Miscellanea di storia dell'arte in onore di J. B. Supino* (Florence, 1933)

RAGGHIANTI, C. R.: 'Scultura lignea senese', *Critica d'Arte* VIII (1949–50), 480*ff.*
'La Madonna eburnea di Giovanni Pisano', *Critica d'Arte* 4 (1954)
'Andrea e Nino Pisano', *Critica d'Arte* 4 (1957)

REEVES, MARJORIE: *The Influence of Prophecy in the Later Middle Ages* (Oxford, 1968)

ROSSI, A.: 'Le sibille nelle arti figurative italiane', *Arte* 18 (1915), 272*ff.*

RUDRAUF, L.: 'The Annunciation. A study of a plastic theme and its variations in painting and sculpture', *Journal of Aesthetics* VII, (1948–49), 325*ff.*

RUSSOLI, F.: 'Una scultura inedita di Giovanni Pisano', *Belle Arti* I (1946–47), 55*ff.*

SANPAOLESI, P.: *Il Duomo di Pisa* (Florence, 1965)

SAUERLANDT, MAX: *Über die Bildwerke des Giovanni Pisano* (Düsseldorf, 1964)

SCHMARSOW, A.: *Italienische Kunst im Zeitalter Dantes* (Augsburg, 1928)

SEDLMAYR, H.: *Die Entstehung der Kathedrale* (Zurich, 1950). Particularly the chapter 'Italien und die Kathedrale', pp. 451*ff.*

SEIDEL, M.: *Giovanni Pisano; Il pulpito di Pistoia* (Florence, 1965)
'Ein neu entdecktes Fragment des genoveser Grabmals der Königin Margarethe von Giovanni Pisano', *Pantheon* XXXVI, 5 (1968)

SERRA, L.: 'La mostra dell'antica arte italiana a Parigi', *Bolletino d'arte* 29 (1935), 30*ff.*

SEZNEC, J.: *The Survival of the Pagan Gods* (New York, 1961)

SIMSON, O. G. VON: *The Gothic Cathedral* (London, 1956)

STEFANINI, P.: 'Il significato simbolico del Pergamo di Giovanni Pisano nella Primaziale di Pisa', *Fede e Arti* III, 11 (1955), 326*ff.*

SUPINO, J. B.: 'Il pergamo di Giovanni Pisano nel duomo di Pisa', *Arch. stor. dell'arte* (1892), 65*ff.*
'Il pulpito di Giovanni Pisano nel museo civico di Pisa', *Arte e storia* (1894), 107*f.*
Arte Pisana (Pisa, 1904)

SWARZENSKI, G.: 'Neuere Literatur über Giovanni Pisano', *Kunstgeschichtliche Anzeigen* (1905), 32*ff.*
Niccolo Pisano (Frankfurt a/M, 1926)

TANFANI, L.: *Sulla ricomposizione del pulpito di Giovanni Pisano* (Pisa, 1873). Report by the commission of the Pisa municipal council.

THIEME AND BECKER: *Allgemeines Lexikon der bildenden Künstler* XXVII, 99–101, *s. v.* 'Giovanni Pisano'. Article by Wolfgang Stechow (Leipzig, 1933)

THOMPSON, BARD: *Patristic Use of the Sibylline Oracles* (Oxford, 1952)

TOESCA, I.: *Andrea e Nino Pisano* (Florence, 1950)

TOESCA, P.: *Storia dell'arte italiana* Vol. II: *Il Trecento* (Turin, 1951), 219*ff.*

TOLAINI, E.: 'Su alcune statue dell' Oratorio di S. Maria della Spina', *Belle Arti* I (1946–47), 39*ff.*

'Aggiunta al catalogo di un seguace di Giovanni Pisano', *Arte figurativa* III (1947), 118*ff.*

TORRETI, P.: 'Una statua della Giustizia di Giovanni Pisano per il monumento di Margarita di Brabante in Genoa', *Commentarii* III, IV (1960)

VALENTINER, W. R.: 'Werke um Giovanni Pisano in Amerika', *Zeitschrift für bildende Kunst* new ser. XXXI (1920), 111*ff.*
'Observations on Sienese and Pisan sculpture', *Art Bulletin* IX (1927)
'The simile in sculptural composition', *Art Quarterly* 10 (1942), 263*ff.*
Tino da Camaino (Paris, 1935)

VASARI, GIORGIO: *Le Vite*, ed. K. G. Frey (Munich, 1911); ed. G. Milanesi (1878)

VENTURI, A.: *Giovanni Pisano* (Bologna, 1928)
'La scuola di Nicola d'Apulia. Impressioni e note', *Arte* 7 (1904), 1*ff.*
Storia dell'arte italiana, Vols. III and IV (1903, 1905)
'Le arte figurative al tempo di Dante', *Arte* 24 (1921), 230*ff.*
'Giovanni Pisano e le Lupedoccioni del Palazzo Pubblico di Siena', *Arte* 26 (1923), 187*ff.*
Giovanni Pisano (Bologna, 1928)

VÖGE, W.: *Die mittelalterlichen Bildwerke in Berliner Museen* (Berlin, n. d.)

'Der Provenzalische Einfluß in Italien', *Rep. f. Kw.* XXV, 409*ff.*

WALLACE, R. D.: *L'influence de la France gotique sur deux des précurseurs de la renaissance italienne: Nicola et Giovanni Pisano* (Geneva, 1953)

WEINBERGER, M.: 'Remarks on the technique of the master's workshop', *Burlington Magazine* LXX (1937), 54*ff.*
'Die Madonna am Nordportal von Notre Dame', *Zeitschrift für bildende Kunst* LXIV (1930–33)
'Giovanni Pisano. A new discovery', *Burlington Magazine*
'Eine Madonna von Giovanni Pisano', *Jahrbuch der Preußischen Kunstsamml.* 51, II–III (1930)

WEISSE, G.: *Die geistige Welt der Gotik und ihre Bedeutung für Italien* (Halle a. d. Saale, 1939)
'L'arte tedesca contemporane a Nicola e Giovanni Pisano', *Arte* 45 (1942), 107*ff.*

WHITE, J.: *Art and Architecture in Italy, 1250–1400* (Pelican History of Art, Harmondsworth, 1966)

YBL, E.: 'Die zwei älteren Pisani und Brunelleschi', *Phoebus* I (1946)

ZAUNER, F. P.: *Die Kanzeln Toskanas aus der romanischen Stilperiode* (Thesis; Munich, 1915)

Index Figures and letters in **bold** type refer to plate and figure numbers